Shining a Light on Grief

real women sharing
real stories of love & loss

compiled by

SUSAN LATAILLE

Shining a Light on Grief:
Real Women Sharing
Real Stories of Love & Loss
Copyright © 2022 Susan Lataille

Produced and printed by Stillwater River Publications.
All rights reserved. Written and produced in the
United States of America. This book may not be reproduced
or sold in any form without the expressed, written
permission of the author(s) and publisher.

Visit our website at
www.StillwaterPress.com
for more information.

First Stillwater River Publications Edition

ISBN: 978-1-958217-19-1

Library of Congress Control Number: 2022910540

Names: Lataille, Susan, compiler.

Title: Shining a light on grief : real women sharing real
stories of love & loss / compiled by Susan

Lataille.

Description: First Stillwater River Publications edition. |
Pawtucket, RI, USA : Stillwater River
Publications, [2022]
Identifiers: ISBN: 978-1-958217-19-1 | LCCN:
2022910540
Subjects: LCSH: Grief--Literary collections. | Grief--
Anecdotes. | Loss (Psychology)--Literary
collections. | Loss (Psychology)--Anecdotes. | Women--
Psychology--Literary collections. |
Women--Psychology--Anecdotes. | LCGFT: Anecdotes.
Classification: LCC: BF575.G7 S45 2022 | DDC:
155.937/02--dc23
1 2 3 4 5 6 7 8 9 10
Compiled by Susan Lataille
Cover & interior book design by Matthew St. Jean
Published by Stillwater River Publications,
Pawtucket, RI, USA.

SHINING A LIGHT
ON GRIEF

Contents

Introduction

by Susan Lataille

It's so easy to feel like we are alone when we are grieving. It was for that reason that I decided to produce this book. The eleven authors who so willingly shared their personal stories of grief on these pages are so very different, yet they have so much in common. I am grateful to each and every one for their courage and honesty, and for showing us all that we are never alone when we face the tragic loss of a loved one.

Shining a Light on Grief speaks from the heart. It is designed to offer hope, inspiration, and comfort, not only to those who are grieving, but for anyone who has lost someone they love, or even perhaps for those who may be sitting alongside a loved one nearing the moment of their own passing.

Through these stories, it is my hope that we can bring the act of grieving into the open. In a world where death and grief are taboo subjects, I believe it is important to share these real, heartfelt stories. It's vital to allow ourselves to feel all the emotions because the only way to heal is to go through the heart of grief and all that comes with it. We all need to recognize that grief, like death, is a natural and normal part of life. It shouldn't be hidden or ignored. It is an integral part of the complete human experience.

It has been five years since the passing of my son Nathan. I love talking about Nathan whenever I have the chance. Celebrating his life and remembering the joy he brought me always brings with it a profound sense of peace.

But on the five-year anniversary, his absence hit me much harder than I thought it would. I found that all the raw emotion was still there, even after all this time had passed. Yet, while I was able to smile and celebrate him, I still felt my heart breaking into a million pieces all over again.

So much has happened over these last five years. As I continue to process my own grief, I have learned so much more about myself. The feelings are mixed—some days, I'm happy, and then there are sudden moments of grief that hit when I least expect it. Other times, I wonder where the joy went, and I have learned to act and do some type of movement or activity to shake up my feelings. Meditation and journaling are two tools I use that I have found help me quite a lot.

Since Nathan's death, I have been guided to help others process their own grief. One of the things I tell my clients is that we are all different and we all grieve in our own unique way. Simply figure out what works for you and do it. Never allow anyone else to tell you how to grieve. Never forget that this is your journey and that it is an inside job—grief needs to be processed on a deep, individual level. It's a personal thing, but it should not be hidden. Sometimes we have to ask for what we need from our friends and loved ones because others may not be able to understand or know what to do or say. We all need to know that it's okay to express yourself and share your needs with them.

Even my own family members were afraid to bring up my son in conversation. I've told them over and over not to worry—I love remembering him. I love hearing all the stories. Today, I am able to bring him up much more often. I believe that he's very much still with me. Love is eternal. Our connection is eternal. Love never dies. I am still a mom and Nathan and I still have a relationship, it's just different now.

Even after five years, I continue to discover who I am without my son. For example, I have learned that one of my superpowers is to help others along their own journey of grief. I enjoy being of service. I enjoy coaching others through their grief. And there have been other realizations, too. I remembered that I love to cook! I love being creative! I love being in nature and going on hikes! I've learned to love myself and my life—all of it, including the grief, the sorrow, the joy, the laughter, the giving and receiving, the help and helping, the asking and the giving…and so much more.

We have to love ourselves enough to continue to live life fully. Life is, after all, for the living. We must find happiness in what we do and what we can create. And connecting to others is important so that we don't feel alone. Sharing our own deeply personal stories of grief can be difficult, which is why I so admire the contributors to this book. When we are able to voice what we're going through to someone who listens, the results for both can be both useful and profound.

My hope is that you, the reader, find the hope and inspiration you need from each chapter of this book to live your life fully with an open heart.

Warning: a box of tissues may be necessary while reading each chapter.

About the Authors

Diane M. Caine

I'm Glad I Didn't Miss the Dance

When you are twenty-something and you have your whole life ahead of you, that's exactly what you think: you have your whole life ahead of you. You have plans and believe that the fairy tale you imagined will play out exactly how you imagine it. Why would you believe otherwise?

That is exactly what Glenn and I thought as we were making our plans for the future. No one would have predicted that a car accident would change *everything*.

My favorite book says, "I know the plans I have for you. Plans to prosper you and not to harm you, plans for a future and a hope." This quote has been the anchor for my life, starting with Glenn's accident, then navigating a painful divorce, raising two daughters as a single mother, finding my keeper husband, Bobby, and blending in his two sons to create our own version of the Brady Bunch.

I chose to share my story when Susan asked me because losing someone so significant at such a young age in adulthood can make or break the rest of your life. I could have gone a completely different path, a path of self-destruction rather than one of self-discovery. I hope to encourage you, the reader, to fully embrace the healing process, to learn something that will bring you comfort and inspire you to enjoy this dance of life.

Diane is the founder and chief empowerment officer of LinkRI, a leadership and human behavior consulting business. She has over twenty years of leadership experience, leading global teams. She is a graduate of Johnson & Wales University. A lifelong learner, she also holds several certifications: DISC Human Behavior Consultant, Maxwell Leadership Executive certified trainer, speaker and coach, Six Sigma Green Belt, Reiki I practitioner, and Magnified Healing initiated master teacher. Helping equip leaders is her passion.

Diane lives in Glocester, Rhode Island with her husband, Bobby. They enjoy weekends playing with their grandbabies when they aren't serving in the community.

Connect with Diane at **www.link-ri.com**.

Wendy Juergens

A Mother and Her Son

This story is about the unique connection between a mother and her son, what the mother learned about herself after her son's death, and what she continues to learn. Wendy wanted to share this story hoping to help others who have lost a loved one to suicide. Upon learning of her son's death, she immediately felt compelled to carry on with his hidden ambition to live a full, laughter-filled life, and influence others to do the same.

Wendy lives in Norton, Massachusetts and is married to her husband, Buddy. Wendy is very proud of her two sons, who both joined the military out of high school, and both achieved non-commissioned officer status during their enlistment. Wendy has two beautiful grandchildren and is also the mom of her furbaby Briggs, an English Mastiff. She has been in direct sales for nineteen years with Reliv International, a nutritional epigenetic supplement company. Wendy enjoys reading, home decorating, and spending time with her husband who has been incredibly supportive and is always able to make her laugh.

Blog: **wendyjuergens.com**
Email: **wendy@wendyandbuddy.biz**
Biz: **https://wendyandbuddy.biz**

Lisa Medley

The Year of Dad

This story is about a year-long journey of a daughter who loves her dad through hospital, hospice, and cleaning out his house. She gets introduced to riding the waves of grief, sometimes gliding gracefully and other times flailing and falling. She discovers that grief is like a wild animal that comes and goes as it pleases. Through the powerful, and sometimes surprising, presence of grief, she learns to give it the respect it deserves. The importance of holistic self-care, emotional healing, and embracing the nonlinear nature of grief are shared. Practical tips are also offered to ease the process of living with grief.

I shared my story because grief needs a voice. The stories in *Shining a Light on Grief* provide a powerful platform for readers to remember the personal and universal nature of grief. Our culture lacks sufficient guidance as to how to heal through grief; not just "get over it." It is not well-versed in the qualities of feeling, being, and releasing. For hundreds and thousands of years, the value of living has been placed on thinking, doing, and controlling. Grief breaks through all those paradigms. This natural emotion implores us to give it time and space, so that we can remain fully alive. Since every human is eventually touched by grief, more sacred spaces are needed to navigate this complex experience. This book offers an avenue of support to remind you to feel, heal, and know that you are not alone.

Losing a loved one is painful. There is no getting around it. My dad's death initiated me into a depth of heartbreak that I had not yet known. Although I would not have voluntarily signed up for this experience, I now have more compassion for myself and others. When Susan asked me to be part of this compilation, I said "yes." There were many times in the writing process that I wanted to change my mind. I had to dig deep, breathe a lot, and just keep going. This is what grief asks of us. I was also inspired by Susan's vision and the beautiful, brave writers who I share this creation with. I appreciate the opportunity to speak to the poignant presence of grief in all our lives. May you find perspectives to inspire you, grace to comfort you, and hope to sustain you.

Lisa Medley helps people reclaim their birthright to feel more connected, comfortable, and confident in their own skin. She is a personal energy optimizer, body relationship expert, and embodiment passionista. Learn more at **www.SoulisticArts.com**

Elizabeth Phinney

But We Were Going to be Bitchy Old Ladies Together…

The first time I experienced death was when I was eleven. I can see the exact moment: my mom got home from work and opened the back door. I was standing in the doorway of the kitchen and said, "I've been trying to call you. Where were you?" She looked at me and so sadly said, "Auntie Tootie died." She burst into tears—I had never seen my mother cry before.

After that, as I got older and into adulthood, older family would die, which you expect. But no one that close to me, so death was always on the outside. My dad died seventeen years ago, but he was older and ailing, so death was almost a gift. Then in 2009, I lost my son. THAT was a complete devastation. I never knew how strong I was supposed to be for the rest of my life until that moment.

My friend who died just two years ago was a whole other matter regarding my connection to death. Losing a best friend leaves a void that can't be filled until that relationship is created with another individual. And that will take time.

Losing my "go-to" person is a daily, often several times a day, loss, over and over again. Someone who you easily text to tell them something funny or hear from them and respond with some clever ditty. Someone who you joked with about being bitchy old ladies together and laughing all the way. And, because she was also my business coach, she knew my professional hopes and dreams and understood and supported them and guided me to help define them. To lose THAT person is overwhelming at times.

I wanted to share my story with Elaine because her death was not something I ever envisioned or even thought about. Losing parents or older relatives is expected. Acquaintances throughout life is just a part of life. Losing a child is every parents' worst fear. But losing a best friend is just not something that ever crossed my mind. I was so taken aback by her death that when this book project came up, I knew instantly that it was Elaine I wanted to write about. I am blessed to still have her in my life every day. Her picture is on my desk, and I glance at it at least a dozen times a day and keep her appraised of what is going on. Because I speak with her and include her, she is still very much a part of my life. So, I know when I am sitting on my back deck with a glass of wine in my hand and start thinking catty thoughts that she is right there beside me laughing and loving.

Elizabeth Phinney is the author of the upcoming book *Thrive to 95 and Beyond* and an expert at Fitness After Forty Five™. You can find her at www.fitnessafterfortyfive.com

Joanne Sapers

Healing Abuse Opens Your Heart to Unconditional Love

My story is about the gifts that came to me by being willing to forgive the perpetrator, forgive my parents, and forgive myself. I lived decades as a victim, numbing my feelings, choosing unhealthy men to love, and feeling unworthy. My life today is magnificent. It is a gift to live each day from a place of serving from my heart and helping women learn how to love themselves unconditionally.

I feel so grateful to be part of Susan Lataille's book. Susan helped me and all the authors feel safe sharing our grief and healing journey. The message I want to convey from my chapter is that it is possible to heal from sexual abuse. I hope that my true story helps you forgive yourself and others, heal, and celebrate who you are. May you know that you are unconditional love, and it is your birthright to be happy, healthy, and free.

I was born in Newton, Massachusetts, then went to college at Massachusetts College and earned an Art BFA. I held the position of sales and marketing for Fortune 500 companies and institutions for ten years. I'm a Reiki master and studied cranial sacral. I have completed over thirty physical and emotional self-development programs. I was the director of administrations for an online spiritual institute for ten years. I'm a certified coach through Life Mastery Institute with Mary Morrissey since 2014, licensed spiritual practitioner through Center for Spiritual Living from 2017-2020, and a lifetime spiritual practitioner.

My business is Pathways to Relationships. I help women over fifty attract the man that loves you for you! I would love to have a conversation with you and learn how I may help you. You can find me contact me at **joanne@pathwaystorelationships.com** or learn more about me at **www.pathwaystorelationships.com/**

Joanne Sapers brings you her love of love and love, which came from her life experiences, combining over thirty years of studies, certifications, and degree programs. Joanne loves being a love relationship coach, a lifetime spiritual practitioner, a speaker, and she is currently writing a book about healthy emotional love and loving.

Carleen DeSisto

My Journey into the Unknown

My story is about what life threw at me after my husband of twenty-seven years was diagnosed with stage four lung cancer. It begins with the diagnosis and how the news affected me personally. I explain why I knew at that moment that my life would be forever changed. I talk about how I felt watching my best friend and love of my life deteriorate so rapidly over a short period of time. I share my opinion on outside support groups and why I chose not to participate in them. Throughout the chapter, I describe my emotional journeys while he was being treated, after his death, and up to the present. My story describes in detail what I learned about myself and the inner strength that came to the surface. It's about having to make difficult decisions and how those decisions affect the rest of your life. It's about giving yourself permission to move on.

I wanted to share my story of how grief affected me and the lessons I learned along the way. I hope that by sharing my experiences, I will be able help others who have lost a loved one deal with their pain and guilt. I wanted to share how important a role that family and a few close friends played in my life in dealing with grief. If my story brings some light and hope to others by describing what I went through and where I am today, it was well worth sharing it. I believe that you can find happiness again if you give yourself permission. It's all about you.

Carleen worked in the investment services industry for twenty-seven years. Her position was terminated in December of 2009 during the recession, eleven months after the passing of her husband. She started her passion career in 2010 as an interior decorator with Décor & You. She has a Bachelor of Science in Business Administration/Management from Bryant University and completed the Interior Design Program at Rhode Island School of Design while working full time and taking night classes. She is passionate about helping her clients create and "love the space they are in." She is blessed with her parents, three siblings, nieces and nephews, and great nieces and great nephews!

cdesisto@decorandyou.com
teamdesisto.decorandyou.com

Catherine DeOrsey

The Hard Way

This story is about the mind body connection with grief. I learned about this connection the hard way. Through three losses and thirty years of stress, I didn't take care of my mental, emotional, and spiritual needs. I took care of everyone else first and didn't take care of myself. I'm a strong person and always thought I was fine. Little did I know, I would suffer the consequences one day.

The loss of my father, my brother, and my friend came crashing down on me when my stomach started to hurt in 2016. Out of nowhere I was diagnosed with a severe autoimmune disease. Through my pain, I learned I wasn't alone and there was a plan behind the plan. To heal my health crisis, one of the areas I needed to address in my life was grief. I finally learned what grief was and processed the pain and suffering I kept inside for so long. My journey to healing wasn't easy but going through the process of releasing grief's pain has freed negative energy from my body, mind, and spirit that was stuck inside for years. Gratefully and thankfully, I am now healed! I've been off all medications for over four years and my MRI continues to show no evidence of disease. Through my continued dedication to self-care for my body, mind, and spirit, I've been able to maintain my health and well-being. I now think about my lost loved ones with love rather than the pain I felt for so long.

I share my story because I never want anyone to have to go through what I did. I want people to take care of themselves especially when they lose someone they love. I don't want people to fear grief. I want people to go through the grieving process in a gentler and easier way than I did.

Through my healing journey I became a certified health coach and went on to create a non-profit to help people get well, stay well, and be well. Integrative Healthcare Solutions is a 501©(3) organization. Our website is **www.ihsri.org**. The mission of Integrative Healthcare Solutions (IHS) is to advance health and wellness by empowering people to take care of themselves. IHS is a resource center that gives people what they need to be well. We provide personalized support and access to services that address the "whole" person. Our goal is to help people create balance in body, mind, and spirit that can be sustained across their lifetime.

Patrice McKinley

A Caregiver's Story

This is a story of one woman's journey caring for a spouse with a terminal illness. When most of us think of the word grief we think of the unfathomable sadness that comes from losing someone we love. But what do you call it when you're caring for and watching that loved one suffer through a terminal illness that spans nearly a decade?

My story is an honest account of the well of emotions that I travelled through during my husband's ten-year battle with prostate cancer and my search to find support for myself while being there for him 24/7. How could I share the guilt of even needing that support? Or of wanting to run away from it all every other day? The fear of not being able to help him and the hopelessness of what was impending was nearly unbearable. How did I dare have feelings myself when my husband was the one who was sick and suffering? It wasn't until I started writing this chapter that I found out about the profound emotions attached to "anticipatory grief." The eventual realization that everything I was feeling was normal and understandable is what I wish for you. It is my heartfelt desire that while reading my story you come to know, with certainty, that you are not alone.

Patrice has been a certified success and personal development coach for the past fifteen years. She is also a professional singer who has produced several one-woman cabaret shows performing them in New York, Boston, and Rhode Island. Through her coaching work and her shows, Patrice is committed to inspiring people to step out and live a life they truly love. She lives in Rhode Island with her wonderful daughters Julia and Micaela. You can contact Patrice at: **expectingresults@patricemckinley.com**

Carrie Beers

Diane is Dancing in Heaven!

I was finally starting to live my life again when the pandemic derailed everything. My sister Diane had been fighting her health nightmare for years, but in late 2019 she insisted I stop waiting to live out a life-long dream I had been preparing for when her health began failing. It was her words that forced me into action to embark on my dream and leave her. Shortly after leaving, the pandemic hit, and her health took a drastic turn. I believe the harsh no-visitor protocols of COVID contributed to my sister losing her will to fight.

My story talks about the emotional rollercoaster I went through during the time I helped in caring for my sister, the challenges I faced trying to get back to her at the height of the pandemic, and how I am healing and grieving with my sister's death.

The decision to write this story was difficult because it had only been a year since her death. I almost stopped but kept writing for two reasons.

First, writing this story was therapeutic, and I discovered the source of my anger since her death. It was not the reason I thought.

The second and original reason I chose to share my story is personal. I have lost and grieved too many loved ones. Each time my experience with grief was different. The one common thread was there was no standard timeline or guideline to process all the emotions and stages of grief we hear about. I grieved each person as uniquely as our relationship was, and to me, that is the perfect way to grieve.

During each grief process at least one person questioned the way I was "doing grief." I even had a CEO ready to withdraw a promotion he had just given me because he thought I was too emotional. He made this decision just months after my sister Beverly died suddenly. Fortunately, he did not withdraw my promotion.

This past year I questioned myself on how I was grieving Diane. Afterall, she had been sick for so long. I should have been prepared; it should not have hurt so much. Feeling this way just added to my emotional turmoil. Then it hit me: it is impossible to prepare for someone leaving your life until they are no longer physically with you.

I am passionate about helping people discover themselves. For the last twenty years I have built my business as a coach, trainer, mentor, and speaker working with clients worldwide. I created The C.O.A.C.H. Principles Leadership System to achieve my mission to make trust, happiness, communication, and inclusion the core values in everyone's life and workplace. My philosophy is simple: BE your best C.O.A.C.H. so you can DO your best! Feel free to reach out to me at **cbeers0830@gmail.com**.

Barbara (Skurka) Barry

How Grief Can Lead to Joy

How can I possibly go on living when my twenty-six-year-old son has died? That was one of my early reactions after Mike's death. Through many resources and tremendous support from family and friends, especially my husband and our daughter, I have learned to live with my heartache and even to rediscover joy and wonder. It has helped me immensely to recognize the things that really matter, and to let go of the rest. I hope that my story can inspire and encourage other grieving moms and suicide loss survivors on their grief journeys.

Barbara Barry loves to connect with people, share her positive attitude about life, and help them communicate effectively, especially with their loved ones. She has made a career as a technology solution-finder, teacher, and business owner. She offers one-on-one coaching through Barry Basic Computer Coaching. Happily married since 1983, Barb and her husband John have two grown children. With their son in heaven, they have begun a new life in Maryland near their wonderful daughter and her family. As they relaunch (not retire!), they enjoy adventuring together, serving their community, exploring their new home state, and traveling.

barbara@barrybasic.com

Shining a Light
on Grief

I'm Glad I Didn't Miss the Dance

In loving memory of Glenn Michael Duncan
November 3, 1967 to November 2, 1992

by Diane M. Caine

I step into the clawfoot bathtub; the porcelain is cold beneath my feet. The hot water runs over my head down my body. It feels comforting, and it helps me get warm. I haven't stopped shaking since we left the hospital on Monday. A day hasn't passed that tears don't stream down my face. Even now standing in the shower on Saturday morning, they crop up. I still can't fathom that today we are burying you. It all still feels like a nightmare. It IS a nightmare.

I turn my face into the water letting it wash away the salt that has accumulated from my tears when I feel the warmth on my shoulders. It's been grey and cold for days, and now today, the sun is shining directly through the bathroom window on me. I turn toward it to allow its warmth to shine on my face. A calming peace washes over me. I feel your presence with me, assuring me that all is well, all will be well, and you surely are playing with the angels, watching over me. I feel you whisper in my ear, "I love you, Precious," and kiss my cheek.

Our Story

Glenn and I met at Johnson & Wales University (JWU). He was in his sophomore year pursuing his Bachelor of Science in Marketing. I was a freshman pursuing my Bachelor of Science in Business Management. Our paths first crossed taking an economics class. A bunch of us in the class started hanging out between classes. Somewhere along the way I started dating another guy in our class and I introduced Glenn to my cousin Jenny. We did some double dates, hanging out—you know the usual college life. It was in the hanging out together you discover compatibility or incompatibility.

After a few months, those initial relationships fell into the incompatible category. Glenn and I still hung out with the rest of the circle of our friends—Kim, Bill, Robin. We wound up in statistics together the following trimester. I secretly (so I thought) shared with Robin that I thought Glenn was cute. I wasn't really sure why Jenny wasn't interested; he was a total catch, in my humble worldly nineteen-year-old opinion.

Robin, who was already engaged to be married, owned a house with her fiancé and invited me to the wedding, was the QUEEN of matchmaking. She decided that it would be a GOOD IDEA standing at the corner of Weybossett Street and Pine Street in downtown Providence—where HUNDREDS of us were walking between campus buildings heading to our next class—to YELL to Glenn who was heading down the street in the opposite direction, "Hey Glenn! Diane thinks you are cute!" My mouth dropped open, I turned one thousand shades of red, turned to her and said, "Oh my GOD, I'm going to KILL YOU!"

Robin's smile was as huge as a Cheshire Cat, Bill was laughing hysterically, and Kim was trying to console me. Glenn turned around, we made eye contact, and he smiled a smile that melted my heart.

We started chatting on the phone and between classes. We had our first date April 1, 1990 (yep, April Fool's Day—to be honest I questioned whether he would come or not, but he did!). We went to dinner at Hemenway's, and he introduced me to comedian George Carlin, who was doing his standup routine at Providence Performing Arts Center (PPAC). We had a great time. As we exited PPAC, he reached for my hand and the connection sent an electric current through my arm. Yes, this was magical, it was the beginning of something special.

Glenn was from Bristol, Connecticut which was two hours from Providence and ninety minutes from my home. His mom was a native Rhode Islander and he lived with his Grammy in East Providence while going to JWU. We saw each other every day between classes, on the nights we weren't working we'd study together, and on the weekends we'd go out. The first time he took me home to Bristol to meet his parents was just before going home for the summer.

And so, it began—the weekend treks between Connecticut and Rhode Island. The summers were long. We quickly discovered that phone calls in the 1990s were EXPENSIVE! So, we went to writing letters during the week and alternating weekends to see each other.

We spent the next two years going to school and travelling to racetracks on the weekends—Glenn was a race enthusiast and a member of Sports Car Club of America (SCCA). We would work weekends at various racetracks as corner workers. There is a ton that goes on behind the scenes of a car race that is not visible to the average fan. We would regularly travel to Limerock Park Raceway, New Hampshire Motor Speedway, Mid-Ohio Sports Car Course, Watkins Glen International, Meadowlands, New Jersey. We worked NASCAR, Indy Car and SCCA events. We had a blast!

Road trips were the place we learned to work together. I was the navigator—I had to learn to read the physical map and get us to where we were going. There were MANY wrong turns and detours—we'd get into spats about reading the map, but eventually figure it out and make it to our destinations. Life was an exciting adventure together!

I knew he was THE one for me. He knew I was THE one for him. He would finish his degree and graduate May 1992. I would graduate with my degree the following May 1993. We started talking about and planning our future the second summer together. We knew it was meant to be forever. We'd already been through two summers of long-distance relationship—another few months wasn't that long. We'd mastered it by the time he graduated.

He returned home to start his new job at Town Fair Tire in Bristol. The plan was we'd continue our alternating weekend treks like we had (when we weren't at a racetrack of course). Our first home would be on the vacant side of his parent's duplex—we had started plotting out what needed to be renovated. We had started planning the wedding. Checking out locations in Bristol since that was going to be our forever home. Choosing colors, who would be in our wedding party. What month did we want to get married in? We chose September 1993.

We celebrated his graduation. We spent our summer traveling to as many races as we could that would fit his schedule. When I started back to school, my work schedule required me to work some Saturday nights. His schedule required him to work some Saturday's during the day. We figured it out. Either one of us would travel on Friday night, sometimes on Saturday afternoon depending on our work schedules. If we didn't spend the entire weekend together at least we had one night and one full day together before going back to work or school.

One particular weekend, my car needed repair. It wasn't going to make the trip to Bristol without me getting stuck. I remember we talked midweek—we would call each other on Wednesday's so we could at least talk (I feel old, but this was before cell phones and texting. We had to pay for long distance calling by the minute—think data charges before you subscribed to your unlimited data plan!). We argued a bit about his coming down even though it was my turn to go there. He had to work during the day, and he'd get to my house after dark—probably around seven or eight—and it would be Halloween night. I would have been able to go on Friday night so we would have had two nights together instead of the one.

At twenty-one, not seeing your future husband for two weeks was catastrophic (we'd already done that when his family took a trip cross country—neither of us did very well not seeing each other for that amount of time!). When you are in love being together is everything!

I also wasn't going to be able to see him ON his birthday, so the weekend was going to be the only time we were able to celebrate his twenty-fifth birthday. He was looking forward to twenty-five. It was an important milestone—his auto insurance rates would finally go down! He could allocate that money to something else—like, you know, renovations, the ring, the wedding.

He arrived early evening Saturday night. We had rituals—he called to say he was leaving, and I knew that he'd be at my door in about ninety minutes time. When he arrived, he called home to report he made it safely. He chatted with his sister Kellie for a couple of minutes, and we spent the evening passing out candy to the few Trick-or-Treaters that came to my parents' house.

We celebrated his birthday at one of his favorite spots—The Grist Mill—on Sunday afternoon. We came back to my parents, and we spent a quiet

Sunday afternoon and evening together looking at wedding magazines, cuddling, planning, and laughing about the stuffed bears he had bought. It was some sort of fundraiser. He bought one for me and one for Kellie. We were having fun goofing around with it. His car was Mazda CX-9, two-door sports car with a little back seat. We talked about how we'd fit a kid in the car, and so, being the funny one, the bear became the back seat passenger for the weekend, all buckled up safe and sound to return home to Kellie.

He stayed later than usual because, you know, two young love birds, the thought of having to leave one another always sucked. They say absence makes the heart grow fonder, and we knew it did. We also were only months away from being together in one spot forever, so we totally cherished the moments we had together with a light at the end of the tunnel soon. He left about 9:30 p.m. knowing he would be home about eleven. He was going to make one stop for gas on the way, then he'd do the ritual one ring when he got home. That was our code for "I'm home safe." It wasn't uncommon for us to leave late evenings.

I walked him to the car. We checked to ensure the bear was safely strapped in the back seat. He put his bag back there too. We lingered a few extra minutes kissing goodbye and soaking in a long embrace. It was time to hit the road. He pulled out, I stood in the doorway watching his taillights disappear, then went inside to get ready for bed and school the next day, waiting for the one ring of the phone...

The Phone Call

It was after 11:00, and I started watching the clock with anticipation. 11:10, 11:15, 11:20...I was starting to get anxious but decided to give him until 11:30. He was stopping for gas on the way home and who knows if there was some unexpected traffic coming through Hartford? Just as I decided 11:30 would be my time to call his house the phone rang. Ahhh relief, he was home...One ring, two rings, three rings, four, I picked up the phone with relief in my voice—"Hi!"

"Diane, it's Kellie."

"Hi, I thought you were Glenn giving me one ring, is he home?"

"Diane, he's not home. He's been in a car accident. The state police just contacted us. He is being taken to Hartford Hospital Trauma Center by helicopter. Mom, Dad, and I are on the way there now. Diane, they said it's pretty bad. I wanted you to know."

My heart dropped into the pit of my stomach, my hands started shaking, tears started to form. I was trying to compute the words she just spoke to me. I think there was a long silence—I really can't remember. I finally found the words. "Oh my God, I'm coming."

By then my mother had made her way to my room. I was up and getting dressed in a state of shock and frankly I don't think very coherent. My mother wanted to know what was going on, my dad had followed behind hearing my raised voice.

"That was Kellie, Glenn's been in an accident. They took him in the HELICOPTER to Hartford Hospital Trauma Center. I'm going!"

My mom was trying to compute, my father was saying I wasn't going, we didn't have a car that would make the trip. I was now bordering on hysterical, screaming, "I'm walking out the door with the damn car, going to the hospital, and YOU CAN'T STOP ME! Did you HEAR ME?! The took him by HELICOPTER! I'm GOING!"

My family was a family of volunteer and professional firefighters. I grew up at the fire station. It was a common occurrence to have life interrupted by the fire pager going off for an emergency. My grandfather, my father, and my brother all would leave the dinner table, jump in the truck, and head to the fire station or directly to the scene of the emergency. I KNOW that when the advanced life support helicopter is coming to the scene that the injuries are life threatening. Time is of the essence for the patient to get to the hospital to be saved.

Everything began to register for my parents. My father was calm and started making a phone call to our family friend to borrow a car. We took my parents' car to our friend's house; we borrowed their van, and we began the longest drive of my life to Hartford. I swear that my father drove the speed limit the entire way and it took us twice the amount of time it should have. We took the wrong exit and wound up having to back track to the hospital. I was beside myself, but also in shock. I don't remember breathing a whole lot—right now my body is tensing up and my breathing is shallow as I write. Here I am thirty years later, and my body remembers it like it was last night.

We FINALLY arrived somewhere close to 1 a.m. and Dad dropped Mom and me at the emergency room door. We walked in, were greeted by a nurse, and then escorted up to the trauma unit by the priest. My knees buckled because I thought we were too late. He and my mom grabbed my arms to support me. Glenn's mother, Maureen, a devote Irish-Catholic, requested a priest come pray with us. Faith was one of our common values. Glenn sponsored me when I decided to be confirmed in the Catholic faith so we could be married in the Catholic church. While I was raised in the Catholic faith, I had not made all my sacraments because at fourteen I wasn't interested.

We arrived on the trauma floor to be greeted by Kellie, Maureen, and Pete (his dad) in the waiting room. Maureen calmly gave me the update that Glenn was in surgery, it was expected to be a few hours. The priest had brought us each a set of rosary beads that the nuns next to the hospital made and distributed to comfort families who were waiting in the trauma unit for their loved ones to recover. He sat and prayed with us. In faith, we expected that the angels were with him, and that God would guide the surgeon and Glenn's injuries would heal.

The sun was starting to rise when the doctor finally came into the waiting room. Glenn was out of surgery, and they were settling him into an ICU room.

She sat with us to calmly tell us his list of injuries:
- A severe head injury with multiple skull fractures
- Left eye socket was broken, there was a question about his ability to see out of the eye
- Left arm was broken
- Left leg was severely broken, so badly they had to amputate it below his knee
- Broken ribs

He had made it through surgery. He was in very critical condition. We would be able to see him, and she warned us he was bandaged pretty much from head to toe.

As she listed the injuries, I was running a check list in my mind:

- Skull fractures, head injuries—bad, long recovery (we can do this)
- Left eye and left leg—ugh, going to impact his driving. Can't push the clutch in—he's going to be pissed about that (we can do this)
- Arm and Ribs—will heal (we can do this)

"Thank you, God, for bringing him through this surgery alive, I know it's a long road ahead. With YOU, Lord, we can do anything."

I remember Maureen very pointedly telling all the staff "this is Diane, this is his fiancée." She was very momma bear about my ability to see him, to be included in conversations and know exactly what was happening with his care. I'm so very grateful that she held me close in that way.

The doctor led us to his room in the ICU. All of us, his parents, my parents, Kellie, and I, were allowed in the room. I was hit by the smell of anesthetics, overwhelmed by the number of machines hooked up to him. He was unrecognizable, like a mummy wrapped from head to toe and swollen in the places that his skin was visible. The only way I could truly know it was him wrapped beneath all the bandages was my high school class ring still on his pinky finger where he always wore it.

The nurses brought me over to his right side so I could hold the one hand that wasn't bandaged and away from all the drains that riddled his body. I was standing next to him, overwhelmed by what I saw and grateful for being able to be with him.

The next thing I knew, Pete was clutching me by my arms, the nurses are swarming around me with smelling salts, and I was trying to figure out what happened. It was all too much to take in and I had fainted. Pete grabbed me before I hit the floor.

The nurses were amazing, they settled me into a chair by his bedside and got me some orange juice. Mom and Dad went back to the waiting room, and so did Pete. Maureen and Kellie made sure I was settled, and the nurses encouraged me to talk to him. To go ahead and touch him and keep talking—he could hear me.

As I started talking to him, his heart rate would go up. The nurse was so excited for me—"See, he does hear you, honey. Keep talking."

So, I did. I stroked his arm talking to him. I teased because I knew stroking his arm like I was stroking a pet used to make him crazy. "I know, honey, that this is probably annoying you, isn't it?" Heart rate up. "Good, I'm going to keep doing it because I know you are paying attention to me." Heart rate up.

"I know that everything hurts and it's a lot of healing, but I'm right here. I love you, and I'm not leaving you." Heart rate up.

I don't remember what else I said other than likely I love you a thousand times. I was able to stay with him until it was time for shift change.

I kissed his hand, I kissed what I could reach of his bandaged head and whispered, "I'll be right back. I love you." Heart rate up.

Code Blue

We were guided back to the waiting room, a familiar space in just the few hours we were there. All you get to do is wait. Waiting, just sitting, waiting. Trying to wrap our minds around what we just saw. Knowing he isn't out of the woods yet, however, hopeful because we had seen him.

Saw his broken body, heard his heartbeat, touched his swollen skin. He was still with us, broken, but with us. Hope is all you have in that moment.

It was about 9:00 a.m. so I called Town Fair Tire to report Glenn was not going to be at work because he had been in a severe accident. We did not know when he would return to work. His manager was compassionate and supportive.

There is always noise at the hospital. Announcements, people walking around, cleaning…background noise doesn't stop. As I sat back down next to Pete another announcement…"Code Blue, Bliss Seven…Code Blue, Bliss Seven." It was the seven that caught my attention.

"Seven, is that the room number Glenn was in?" I asked Pete.

"I'm not sure," Pete said.

I looked questioningly at Kellie. She nodded yes, but we had no idea what a Code Blue was.

Maureen had gone off with her sister Debbie, a nurse, to get a cup of tea. They were just walking back in the waiting room when the doctor came in to speak to us.

Naturally we were all anxious for an update.

Glenn had gone into cardiac arrest. They worked diligently to revive him; however, his injuries were so severe and the stress on his body was too much. He was gone.

He was gone…those words hung in the air like they were physical things.

I didn't cry immediately; I was fully in a state of shock. Pete put his arm around me and started crying. Debbie was closest to Maureen and grabbed her. I didn't know where Kellie was. I was swirling in my head. The tears came down my face. How could he be gone? No, this wasn't real. He couldn't be gone.

The doctor left and then entered the social worker. Now the administrative parts of death kicked in. We didn't ever see the doctor again; the social worker was kind and compassionate about next steps. We were brought back into another room to see him again. This time it was quiet, the lights were dim, and we gathered around him. The tears seemed endless. I still felt numb, then cold, then hot. It's so weird what your body does when you are in shock. Pete and Kellie left the room. Pete was having a hard time fathoming his first-born son was gone. Kellie was her dad's comfort. Maureen stayed right by my side. She allowed me to stay as long as we could. She held my arm, and we walked together—arm in arm—as the social worker led us to another room to do the paperwork.

We were met by the flight nurse who cared for Glenn in the helicopter. She was so kind and caring. She offered her condolences to us, and she handed us each two pins. One was a Lifestar helicopter pin (God bless them, they do such hard work—every call is a life and death call for them). The other was a butterfly. She explained the significance of it. Butterflies are symbols of transformation, that while he might be gone physically, he was free from the injuries and his soul was free. She pinned the butterfly on me and gave me a hug.

The social worker waited patiently, holding space for the moment, then moved us to the room to process. Maureen had to sign paperwork to release his body to the funeral home.

"Do you know where you would like him taken?"

Maureen responded that his school mate's family owned a funeral home, they would take good care of him.

I sat in witness to all of this, still trying to process what was happening, holding the pin in one hand and the rosary beads in the other, the tears just flowing down my face like little rivers without end.

Prayer Candles, Not Birthday Candles

Instead of celebrating his birth, we were at the funeral home tending to his death.

Instead of choosing wedding invitations, I was choosing prayer cards.

Instead of choosing my wedding dress, I was choosing his burial outfit.

Instead of choosing the colors for our new home, I was choosing the color of his casket.

Instead of choosing a location for our future home, I was choosing a plot in the cemetery where he would be buried.

Instead of lighting candles on his birthday cake, I was at the church lighting a prayer candle for his soul.

Instead of choosing our wedding song, I was choosing music to be played at the funeral.

This wasn't what I was supposed to be doing. This wasn't what we were supposed to be doing. How on earth did I jump from fiancée to widow and miss the wife part? Who pulled the rug out from under me? I just didn't understand!

We had several days between the planning and the funeral. There was family coming from out of state. I stayed with Maureen and Pete the whole time. My parents had come back to bring me clothes for the week and for the funeral. I was NOT going home yet. I had to be where he was. They honored my needs even though I can only imagine how hard it was to leave me there and not be able to take my pain away.

Walking Down the Aisle

You send invitations for the wedding; you choose who gets to share the joy of your day together. You don't send invitations for a funeral—people just show up. The people who come to support you in the darkest, most painful time of your life are the ones who leave the mark on your heart. It's easy to celebrate joyous occasions, it's hard to be with someone who is in the throes of grief. Especially when it's unexpected, especially when "it's not supposed to be this way." Especially when they have not experienced it and don't know how to relate.

You remember who went out of their way to be there with you. I was surprised who showed up: friends from the racetrack travelling hours, my friend Megan from high school who hopped a plane from New York to be by my side, firefighters and police officers from home. That is how a first responder family roles—they stick together in all of it. I knew of the bond, however; I experienced it firsthand that day.

We got into the limo and traveled to the church. I was wearing a black dress, not a wedding dress.

We watched as his casket was carried up the stairs of the church steps and placed at the end of the aisle. I stood waiting, flanked by Maureen and Pete, not on my father's arm like I thought I would be, standing in this spot.

The pall bearers—not his groom's men—wheeled him down the aisle to the altar instead of standing on it with him. I walked down the aisle behind him instead of walking down the aisle TO him. The music was sorrowful, not joyful.

A funeral mass and a wedding mass aren't that different in structure. There are prayers, there is music; yet instead of vows, there are remembrances. Instead of tears of joy, there are tears of grief (although grief is just as present at a wedding as there is at a funeral, it's a different kind). Joy and grief are constant companions—this I have learned.

What I Have Learned

By the time this book is published I will have celebrated my fifty-first birthday. Glenn has been dead longer than he had been alive. Thirty years have passed, and I assure you that even today I can feel his presence as closely as I did the morning of the funeral in the shower. He is with me right now as I write.

Let that sink in for a moment—*Thirty years*. I have lived longer without him than I did with him, yet he is still very present with me on pretty much a daily basis. As with every person you love, you carry them with you. *Love never fails.* This I KNOW.

I have learned much through the last thirty years of living with grief. Yes, I said *living with grief.* Grief is not an event; it is an emotion. It is part of you, just like every other emotion we feel—love, anger, joy, sorrow, laughter, and tears. They come in waves, some big, some small. Some you bask in, others you wish would leave quickly. They all come to pass, if you allow yourself to fully feel into them and process through them.

At twenty-one, I did the best I could to cope.

I went to a bereavement support group because I didn't know how to do this, this grieving and living. I attended with my mom and Glenn's Grammy and aunt. I went because I knew Glenn would want me to LIVE *without* him, as much as I did *with* him.

I slept in his hockey jersey every night to be close to him. I slept with and carried that teddy bear he bought me for comfort. It was the last physical piece of him I had.

I wrote him letters and journaled—a coping strategy I learned at bereavement group.

I went back to school the week after the funeral. I chose to finish, because he had been willing to sacrifice for me to complete school and he would have wanted me to. It was also part of the original plan. Sometimes we do what is comfortable and familiar to cope. I graduated in May (six months after the accident), on time with high honors—Magna Cum Laude. School gave me something to focus on besides the pain.

I drank A LOT that summer—sometimes to the point of blacking out and not remembering what I had done. Thankfully, I was surrounded by the family at the fire station—drinking was and still is a coping mechanism for first responders. I was kept safe when I got sloppy drunk.

I tried to return to the racetrack, but I couldn't do it. I did go back to Limerock Park in the fall with Glenn's cousin, so I could show him Glenn's favorite track, but I have not flagged another race.

I spent every weekend for a year going to see his parents and sleeping in his bed when I was there—even after his brother moved it to the attic. It was hard for him to sleep in the same space he had shared with his brother with his brother's things in it.

I eventually dated again; the first date was a longtime friend. He had lost his father in the few months following Glenn's accident, and grief was our common denominator. He was home from the air force on bereavement leave so we spent most of our time together. The first kiss felt like betrayal, and I cried. He was gentle and compassionate with me. He let me cry and just held me. We did a lot of that those few weeks. When he went back on duty, our time together ran its course. Hurt has a funny way of bringing people together to help each other heal in small and big ways.

I had friends who had been close never check on me after the funeral. At first, I was hurt, but now I realize that people just don't know how to handle the pain, the tears; they are afraid to upset you or say the wrong thing. They have something you don't any longer and guilt kicks in. It's not your fault or theirs—death is a scary thing for so many. They are doing the best that they can and so are YOU.

What I want you most to know is that there is no "right" or "wrong" way to grieve. There are, however, healthy and unhealthy choices we make when we are in a state of deep pain that grief brings.

Surround yourself with loving supports—that may come in the form of:
- Wearing an article of clothing
- Sleeping with stuffed animals
- Attending a grief support group
- Visiting your favorite places
- Speaking with a trusted friend who will listen
- Seeking out a therapist
- Taking long walks or working out
- Taking a bath
- Trying out alternative healing methods
- Allowing yourself the full out noisy sobbing cry and even wailing to allow the grief to pass through you
- Giving yourself space to process when an anniversary, birthday, or holiday comes up (especially the first year—the first year is usually the most acutely painful)

The Dance

Glenn's death and life changed me forever. At twenty-one, I knew that life was not guaranteed. That the plans we think we have can be changed in the blink of an eye. I have an entirely different appreciation for the simple things. Glenn taught me to live life to the fullest while we were together.

It also had me living for YEARS with an overwhelming fear of loss. It was a low-level kind of worry playing in the background always. I have rules that my husband and my children must follow or feel my wrath: You don't leave the house without a kiss and hug. You don't leave without hearing the words "I love you."

I had some really screwed up beliefs that the accident was my fault because it was supposed to be my turn to drive to Bristol. I would play all these unhealthy what if games in my head. What if I had driven like I was supposed to? What if I had borrowed a car? What if he just stayed home? He would be alive right now…All unhealthy, all false, and all out of my control.

Grief has many layers to it. Some we can move through quickly, some require therapy—and sometimes many modalities of therapy—some we didn't even realize we passed through until you wake up one day without the pit in your stomach or the ache in your heart. One day grief doesn't consume you, you learn to walk along side of it. You don't fear it, you recognize it as an old friend who is reminding you that you loved greatly—what a blessing—you LOVED.

At the funeral we played "The Dance" by Garth Brooks. To this day, when I hear it, it will bring tears. Now the tears are not filled with pain, only gratitude for having been able to love and be loved unconditionally. If I hadn't lived through his loss, I wouldn't be writing to you, hoping to help you navigate this journey with grief.

I'll share some of the lyrics; I hope they bring you comfort. I hope one day you, too, will smile in gratitude for what you shared with your loved one(s). Remember that their spirit is close to you and love never, never, never dies…

Looking back on the memory of
The dance we shared 'neath the stars above
For a moment all the world was right
How could I have known that you'd ever say goodbye
And now I'm glad I didn't know
The way it all would end, the way it all would go
Our lives are better left to chance
I could have missed the pain
But I'd have had to miss the dance…

CHAPTER 2

A Mother and Her Son

In loving memory of Nicholas "Nick" Bertozzi
September 28, 1979 to May 14, 2012

by Wendy Juergens

My life was turned upside down one Monday evening in May of 2012. It was the night after Mother's Day at 7:30. My husband was taking a shower, and I was in my office listening to voicemail. When you're self-employed, there's always work to be done, but that night became an extraordinary night when our home phone rang, and when something extraordinary happens, it will be instilled in your brain forever. It will always feel like it happened yesterday.

The Monday after Mother's Day in 2012 set the stage for my future Mondays. Nick has been gone close to ten years now. Starting with the Monday after he died, the first day of the week has continued to be a challenging day. When I would have a particularly difficult day, whether dealing with emotions or just having a rotten day, my husband would always remind me, "Remember, it's Monday."

This story will start with the day Nick took his life. For me, it was a very strange, awkward day. I started the day with my husband, Buddy, by going to a local restaurant for coffee and a light breakfast. That was the norm for us. But this Monday felt different somehow. When we left the restaurant, Buddy headed out to start his workday and I headed to my home office. Sitting at my desk, I looked upon a stack of paper, bills to pay, calls to make. But that's all I could do—look at it. There was some-thing wrong. I was ill at ease which caused me some distress. I had heard a joke on the radio on my way home from breakfast. It was the type of joke Nick and I would laugh about. I texted the joke to Nick and asked him, "Do you think Buddy will think it's funny? How about Cathy?" Cathy is a friend of mine who sometimes expresses concerned over my black humor. He got back to me and said he also thought it was funny and asked me to let him know what Buddy and Cathy thought. We'd compare notes.

As the day went on, I was having more and more difficulty concentrating. It felt like an out-of-body experience. Finally, around 2:30 that afternoon, I decided to grab a book I was reading for book club and head out to a coffee shop. It was quite evident that I was not going to get any work done that day.

I picked up my book, grabbed my keys and pocketbook off the desk. Before heading out, I went down to our TV room where my dogs were lounging the day away. I always say goodbye to my pups and get a little wag of the tails in response. I was driving a Mini Cooper at the time. It was a fairly new car to me. We had recently introduced the car to Nick when we picked him up to go to dinner. He was sitting in the back seat expressing surprise at the spaciousness of it, but I will never forget his comment once we were on the road and after a few minutes sitting in silence.

"You know what this car reminds me of?"

"No, what?"

He went on to say, "It reminds me of an urban assault vehicle!"

I will admit that you did "feel the road" in that car. We named the car Tank that night.

A few minutes after leaving the house that Monday afternoon, I was on the highway. My brain still was not engaging. It is so difficult to describe how I was feeling or thinking, or not thinking—most definitely not focusing. My thoughts were complex and at the same time unavailable to me. It started to rain. Was it supposed to rain that afternoon? Then about ten minutes into my drive, I suddenly realized that I lost track of where I was. Had I passed the exit? Between the rain and being in a very small car, I quickly decided that the best and safest thing for me to do was to get off the highway. I felt so disoriented, and for some reason I felt like crying. My mind was somewhere else. It was as though something or someone was interfering with my thought processes. Uneasiness prevailed.

Finally, I found a place to exit the highway safely. I realized then that I had passed the exit to the coffee shop. Now it was pouring rain. I was almost in a panic. The best decision I could make was to slow down my racing mind, to breathe and go home now that I was sure of where I was. I was now feeling safer. I said to myself, "No more highway for me today." A much slower pace, no big trucks spraying me with water, and less traffic—that's what I needed. Next thing I knew, the sun was shining, and I was pulling into my driveway. I stepped into the safety of my home, greeted by the dogs. It's so funny how dogs will act as if they haven't seen you for a week when you've only been gone a few hours. They seemed more excited than usual. I was just glad to be home and have them as a distraction.

About an hour later when my husband arrived home, we were sharing our day's activities with each other. I asked him if he got caught in the rain.

"What rain?" I told him about the heavy rain I got caught in literally down the street from our house. "Nope, it didn't rain where I was."

How could that be? It had poured, and we were in the same vicinity. I was beginning to feel like I was going crazy.

During the time frame of my misadventure that afternoon, my son would have been driving to a packed gravel parking area adjacent to the Boston Providence railroad tracks in Foxboro. He must have been in a psychotic state at that point, in a dark place of hopelessness. Had I been feeling lost, uneasy, at the same time that afternoon?

Days later I wondered if it was raining where Nick had been that afternoon. He loved the rain. One of his shipmates wrote a post on social media about a group of fellow sailors at Pearl Harbor who were standing in a doorway waiting for the rain to stop when Nick strode around the corner of the building. He was soaking wet, boots squishing water with every step. When he saw his coworkers hiding from the rain, he gave them a little smirk and said, "Sometimes you have to walk in the rain." Without missing a step, he continued walking to his quarters. When I was making decisions regarding Nick's headstone, this seemed like the perfect quote to have engraved. Everyone who first sees the quote will comment on it. They do not know the story behind it, but it is the type of quote that will have meaning to all who see it, just like Nick had meaning to everyone he met.

The internet is a wonderful tool. Recently, I looked up the weather for the day I got rained on—May 14, 2012. Come to find out, it was clear and sunny in Foxboro; however, in Plainville, where I happened to be on the highway between sometime between 2:30 and 3:00, it rained! It rained on me until I got to the Foxboro town line. Finding this information made me smile. I've always wondered if it was a message from Nick.

Because I had such a miserable, non-productive day, Buddy suggested we go out and grab a bite to eat before visiting our puppies. Our dog had puppies on Monday the seventh, exactly one week prior. We would go to the breeders' house almost every evening to help, which meant anything from bottle feeding the puppies, holding them, and the fun part, cleaning up after them. I did not realize how messy newborn puppies could be and how much work was involved. We arrived at the breeders' house at around 5:30 p.m. After spending an hour or so with the puppies, we headed home. I was exhausted from my unnerving day. On our way home, I texted Nick to let him know how my husband and friend responded to the joke I texted him earlier. There was no reply, which was unusual for Nick. He always got right back to me. Maybe he got called in to work. Little did we know that just prior to our arrival at the breeders there was an entourage of emergency vehicles that flew by the breeders' house. Fire trucks, police cruisers, and ambulances with sirens blaring and lights flashing headed to the scene of our son's death.

That evening when the chief of police called, I was caught off guard. He said he needed to talk to me, but he didn't have our address. It would take about ten minutes for him to get to our house from where he called. After hanging up, I let Buddy know that the chief was on the way.

Buddy asked why, and I instinctively said, "I think it's Nick." I had no idea where that came from.

"What do you mean you think it's Nick?" He sounded scared and irritated at the same time.

"I think something's happened to Nick. Hurry up and get out of the shower. He'll be here any minute."

A few minutes later there was a knock on the door. I invited the chief and his detective into our office. Buddy and I stood behind the office desk, and the chief and detective stood in front of the desk. Suddenly my legs felt like rubber, my body was tingling all over. Soon I would know why I was feeling this way. Both of my boys enlisted in the military out of high school. I always wondered how I would react if military personnel showed up on my doorstep to give me bad news. What I imagined was magnified a thousand times this night.

The chief said there had been an accident. Nick's car was parked at the accident location, next to the railroad tracks. They had determined that it was Nick's remains by locating his Facebook page and matching his three-quarter sleeve tattoo shown on his profile picture to his arm. They finally got around to telling us he had been struck by a train. Buddy literally fell into the office chair sobbing. I must have been in shock because I continued to stand there staring at the messenger. The chief had to leave. He asked if I could spend some time with the detective to answer some questions. I said, "Sure," and then thanked him for personally coming by to tell us the news.

After spending some time with the detective, Buddy and I looked at each other in disbelief, shaking our heads. Buddy asked me how I could remain so calm when I heard the news. I truly believe that Nick had been communicating with me all day. I told Buddy that when I heard the news, I immediately thought, "Nick has given me a job. I have a very important job to do." I had to stay strong. There would be plenty of time later to bawl my eyes out.

That was the beginning of an extraordinarily emotional journey that I had been secretly dreading for years. I knew Nick had been struggling with depression for a long time and I often worried about something like this happening. Upon hearing the news that evening, my immediate feeling was, "That poor kid." I felt so bad for him, picturing him all alone feeling he needed to leave our world to escape the pain he was in. I did not feel any sense of failure as his mom, but I did feel that I let him down as a human being. He talked to me a few times about his depression. It was so hard to see him crying while telling me how he felt. I will never forget his saying to me, "You're the only person I can trust."

My mother had been in and out of the hospital and nursing home for months prior to Nick's death. I was so preoccupied with her needs that I missed the signs that Nick was giving. One of Nick's friends said he didn't want to bother me because I was so busy with taking care of my mother.

When he left the house on Mother's Day, Buddy said, "Nick doesn't seem himself."

News travels fast! We had a lot of visitors drop by the house that night. The next morning brought even more people, one of whom was the pastor of our church. The pastor had been told that it was a suicide and had no qualms about performing the ceremony. He asked if we could spend some time with him. He wanted to learn more about Nick. When the pastor stood to leave, he said that he regretted never having met Nick.

Within a couple of days, I contacted a local attorney who assigned me the personal representative of Nick's personal affects and assets. How I got through these days it nothing short of a miracle. My world was changing second by second, minute by minute. Time seemed to be racing by in those early days yet at times it felt as though time was standing still. I was still convinced that Nick had assigned me a job—that he knew I could handle this. My role as personal representative felt more like a roller coaster ride than an administrative role.

The funeral home was one block out of the center of town. Because of the location, I would drive by many times in the next few weeks. Our first visit was to discuss arrangements. My husband and I knew the funeral director personally, and she happened to know Nick because he was a funeral director. He had once worked for her cousin's funeral home, so the difficult conversation about arrangements was buffered by working with a good friend who had a relationship with Nick.

The funeral was going to be delayed a few days. Nick's body had been sent to the medical examiner's office in Boston to be officially identified and to determine the cause of death. When Nick was taking funeral services courses and later when he got his first job with a funeral home, we talked about the different aspects of funeral services. It is a very interesting profession. When he first talked about suicides, the first statement he made was, "How bad could things be" that someone would take their own life. It is so sad to know that he discovered how bad things could be, how much pain one suffers.

The funeral director was wonderful. I could drop by the funeral home at any time. She would sit with me and listen to me talk about Nick, family members, the process—anything. She called me the day they were going to Boston to pick up Nick's body. My grieving started all over again. I was totally caught off guard. Of course, I knew that day was coming, the day when Nick's body would be back in Foxboro, but it was such a foreign feeling to me. The grief was different; it was a stronger, deeper feeling. It is not as if I had never lost a loved one, because I had lost quite a few; but THIS was my child. It was different—THIS WAS MY BABY.

Hundreds of people attended the wake. I tried to put my emotions aside to be available to the people who came to pay their respects. If I had the time, I would have wanted to hear everyone's story. I was especially curious about the young adults who were there to say good-bye to their thirty-two-year-old friend. How did they know Nick? Where did they meet him? The stories I did hear all ended in "I will never forget him." Hearing these stories made me so proud of the caring man Nick had become.

I visited the funeral home a couple of days before the viewing to ask if we could have a basket available for people to place notes, letters, and other items in the day of the funeral. All the items would be added to Nick's casket. She thought that was a wonderful idea. I added Benji, a stuffed animal that Nick had since he was a toddler. Yes, he had kept Benji all those years. I was curious, so I looked up Benji's history on the internet. He was a rescue dog, just like a role he portrayed in a movie. Later in the year we held a fundraiser for the American Foundation for Suicide Prevention. Because Nick was such a dog lover, the monies from the event were donated to the Mansfield Animal Shelter. This was a very fitting donation.

I thought the basket would help people with their own grieving process, but I also thought Nick would have appreciated it. I likened it to his vehicles that were always filled with clothing, trash, and everything in between. "It would be perfect." She agreed. We ended up with a basketful of items. I was so happy to hear people say that they really enjoyed placing their notes and other items in the basket knowing that they would be with Nick forever. One item that I thought was a remarkable gesture was an alumni ring from the college he was attending. He had become too ill to finish his college degree.

The next day was the funeral. It seemed that a lot of time had passed. Here I was again feeling so disconnected. There were so many people:

relatives, friends, former and current day coworkers, people who treated Nick well and people who did not treat him so well. I am not one to hold a grudge, so all these people were on equal standing with me that day whether they had been kind or hurtful to Nick over the past years. They were there to pay their respects, not cause more harm.

My husband and I followed the flag-draped casket into the church. Six pallbearers guided the casket into place. We were then directed to our seats. It was so surreal. This may sound strange, but I felt Nick's presence there in the church. Memories of conversations he and I had about his experiences working as a funeral director. I had been worried about Nick and his depression for so long. Today, there was no reason to worry. Nick was at peace now. I had set an intention to be in the moment for the service. My attempt to do so was grossly challenged. I wanted so much to remember the experience but had so many emotions tugging at me, pulling me this way and that.

I was recalling that on occasion my husband and I would invite Nick to attend a Sunday service at this same church, thinking that maybe meeting some of our friends would somehow be encouraging to Nick. He would always decline our invitations. With a giggle, he would say, "I go to church almost every day." This was true, but he was not going to church for his own benefit, he was attending as a funeral director. "A little different," I would say. Deep down I know that he knew I was only trying to help him.

As we sat waiting for the service to begin, I looked behind me. The church was full, standing room only. I was happy to see the pastor when he walked down the aisle. This meant the service would begin, that I could now focus on his words. "Stay in the present, Wendy" was the little voice I heard again.

When I first joined the church, I had a meeting with the pastor. I told him about my church history, how going to church was so difficult for me. I started attending church when I was five years old. It was the start of the school year, my kindergarten year. Every Sunday at 8:00 a.m., one of my parents would drop me off in front of the church. I would exit the car and walk into the church all by myself. There were so many things I disliked about my Sunday mornings. What I disliked the most was having to get all dressed up in a dress, hat, and white gloves. This was not me. Other than wearing a skirt to school, my days were spent in dungarees, the present-day jeans, and a flannel shirt or T-shirt depending on the season. Dressing up caused me to feel like a stranger in my own skin. All dressed up for church, I would walk through the huge church doors dragging what little confidence I had behind me. There were a couple of very nice people who would invite me to sit next to them. I imagine they felt bad that I was there all by myself, so young and alone. After the church service, I would attend Sunday school. After Sunday school, I'd exit the church and do a search for my parents' car, again, all alone walking down the sidewalk while everyone else seemed to be enjoying themselves, chatting and saying their goodbyes.

Pastor remembered my story. He had decided against the pomp and circumstance of a formal service. I believe that was for my benefit. He was wearing khakis, his black shirt with white collar, and a sports jacket, and most importantly a smile. Yes, this was a somber event; but I believed that his smile simply represented Nick's personality, as Pastor understood it to be.

All in all, my son's funeral was amazing. Pastor warmly welcomed family and friends. A warmth flowed through the church. It was surreal. After his welcome statement, Pastor immediately talked about suicide. You could have heard a pin drop. He talked about depression being an illness that can lead to suicide. He went on to tell the story of a bishop he studied under who looked down upon suicide. After all, it was a sin! A person who commits suicide does not have an opportunity or time to ask for forgiveness, but we can forgive these souls who were in so much pain. This story took a turn. The bishop in this story lost a niece to suicide. This changed his views on suicide. It was an amazing story—a story of hope. Pastor's words touched everyone in that church.

Nick's brother and Nick's best friend read the eulogy they had written the night before. Again, I felt as though Nick was there with us, laughing at himself as he often did. People in attendance were laughing and then crying, and then laughing again. The eulogy truly described Nick in his truest form. It is a piece I will always treasure. The last paragraph read:

"Nick, I'll forever see you walking toward me—those dull black boots shuffling along with that walk that was all your own, the ratty but proud

Charlotte hat, a tight black tee accentuating the tattoo you designed yourself, or perhaps a long sleeve shirt with the filthiest cuffs imaginable, your
bright brown eyes flashing, and that smile that could light the world.

"Fair winds and following seas, brother."

It was over. It was time to leave, time to follow Nick's casket out of the
church. As we walked down the aisle, I noticed that everyone was wearing
a purple ribbon. These ribbons were made by four young women who con-
sidered Nick family. They handed these ribbons out as people entered the
church that morning. You may have guessed—purple was Nick's favorite
color. Another friend of his made sure all the pallbearers had purple ties
to wear as well.

Watching the casket being guided into the hearse was another strike
at the emotions. I could not believe I was witnessing this. Yes, the casket
only held Nick's remains, but it was a time of heightened emotions for
me, a time of letting go, a time for another layer of realization. Nick's
bright brown eyes would shine no more. He would not be sharing anymore funny stories. There would be no more teasing, no more pranks. The
moments of relief I had been feeling were growing into deep feelings of
loss. I had to keep reminding myself that Nick would no longer have to
fight his demons. He was finally relieved of his extreme emotional pain.

Nick had a way of inserting himself into the families he worked with.
These families thought the world of him. He had an infectious personality
that made people want to be with him. The family with the four daughters called him number five, "the brother they never knew they always
wanted." Another family learned of Nick's dedication through his work
and relationship building. A little three-year-old girl, the granddaughter of
the funeral home owner, saw Nick at work with his handsome features and
well-groomed beard, and she instantly associated him with a prince from
her book of fairytales. From that point on, he became known as "Prince
Nick." Not long after meeting this beautiful little three-year-old, Nick
came across a large basket of princess paraphernalia at a charity auction. He
stayed until he was sure that he had outbid everyone else for that basket.
The next morning, he brought the basket to the little three-year-old.

Nick's funeral was held at a church just down the street from the cemetery and only a couple blocks away from the funeral home. Everything was within close proximity of each other. Even Nick's apartment was close by. He loved his hometown. He often walked to the center of town to get his meals or go to the YMCA. Being a member of the Y, Nick would grab a sub at a local sub shop and take it to the Y, sit in a comfortable chair in the lobby, and watch their big screen TV. He didn't have a TV at the time. A friend of mine told me she saw him sitting with his sandwich watching TV. He gave her a little wave, the type of wave that acknowledged her but also told her to keep moving because he was in the middle of watching a show. No need to stop and talk. He was funny that way.

The final stop on the day of the funeral was the cemetery where a graveside service was held. My mother and her sister were both in wheelchairs. It suddenly hit me that my mother would never see Nick again. He always made her laugh which was hard to do these days. Her dementia stole her emotions on some level. When she found out Nick had died, she said, "It should have been me." She never cried or said anymore about it. I felt so helpless watching her that day.

A coworker of Nick's, who was also a funeral director, requested that he be allowed to take care of placing the flowers over Nick's grave once the casket had been lowered and earth filled in. He and Nick were very close. The funeral director knew this would serve as a piece of closure for him. So many funny stories were shared between them. If you are unfamiliar with funeral director humor, know that it is very different and very respectful at the same time. Nick's coworker made up a grave marker to stick in the ground in front of the flowers. It had all the pertinent information on it: name, date of birth, date of death, and a little quote that read, "Can you smell me yet?" There's that sense of humor I was talking about. Nick would have loved it.

Everyone was invited back to the church for food and socializing. I cannot remember all the people who were there. I was told that two of Nick's "mates" from his submarine days were there. One flew in from Texas and the other from somewhere on the West Coast. I was sorry that I missed a chance to chat with them. It is such a shame that to this day I cannot recall the names of all the people in attendance, but what I do remember is that I was treated with kindness and affection. After a few hours, people started leaving. When we left there were a handful of church members who would stay to clean up. It was time to go home.

I was so thankful for my dogs that day. The greeting I received as I walked through the door helped to cheer me up. We were still waiting for our puppy to come home, so I had that to look forward to. Her mother was already home. The puppy followed in two weeks. That puppy never left my side except to eat or drink. She was quiet and attentive and never got into any mischief. I felt such a strong connection with her. I was to pick out the puppy I wanted. Instead of me picking one, she picked me. A year went by before she started leaving my side. Dogs are very intuitive. She knew I was doing better.

This May will be the tenth anniversary of Nick's death. It still feels like it happened yesterday. Being a suicide survivor adds a twist to grief. I was talking to a friend of mine who lost his brother to suicide. I loved his description of how it felt to him. Picture standing at the edge of the ocean about knee deep. The first wave that hits your knees knocks you over. The second wave, just as strong, almost knocks you over, but you are more prepared. You can handle the third wave more easily as you are getting used to the force or feeling. As the fourth wave approaches, you are even more prepared. You have experienced enough waves to know what is coming and how to stand up to it. Each wave after that is different, some stronger than others. Each year is different. There is no predicting my days. I will say that my memories are mostly happy memories. Sadness will occasionally tap me on the shoulder, but that is okay.

My emotions differed each day. My husband and I owned a business, so talking to people was a necessary part of the job for Buddy. There was no predicting how he or I would feel on any given day. Each day presented different challenges. Personally, I would start the early days of my grief feeling somewhat normal and then suddenly feel a deep sadness, which was usually tied to a memory. Anniversaries were triggers as well. The two-year anniversary for me was worse than the first-year anniversary. There is no explanation for this. No one grieves in the same time frame or with the same degree of emotion. What I realized was that the second anniversary for me felt more like a reality slap, whereas the first year felt somewhat celebratory.

It is difficult to describe how I feel or how I am doing because it changes every day. Thankfully I am much happier accepting the life I have been dealt. I feel so blessed to have found peace in my life, especially now that I am in my "senior" years. Learning to enjoy the simple things in life has saved me.

Writing has been the most therapeutic activity for me. There is a box of stories in my closet that is calling my name. The night Nick died is the night my writing began. I was simply recording my memories which helped me to get through the days and nights following the loss. It helped me to remember fun times with Nick and stories he shared. I also captured what others wrote about Nick.

Memories of your loved ones are important. Sharing those memories with your family and friends when you are all gathered for a holiday or special event is vital to keeping the memories alive. I love talking about Nick, and I enjoy hearing others' stories of his antics. There are a few of us who feel comfortable sharing our stories, and there are others who are still not ready. Everyone grieves in their own way, on their own terms, in their own time. There is no schedule or timeline for grieving. That is why writing has helped me so much.

I was very proud of him and the work he did. His fun-loving ways combined with his dedication to his work provided a perfect combination. Here is a special memory I would like to share. I recall Nick telling us about the first memorial graveside service he participated in. It was a private service for a little boy who had passed. His parents, a priest, Nick, and his employer were present. Nick was charged with bringing balloons to the service and holding them until the family arrived. Once they were all gathered next to the grave, Nick handed five balloons to each family member. The plan was for everyone to release their balloons after the "amen." Everyone followed the plan perfectly, but at that very moment they released the balloons, a gust of wind came from nowhere and blew all the balloons into a nearby tree amongst the branches. The balloons seemed happy to help this little boy send a message to those in attendance. Nick, who was a little boy at heart himself, stared in disbelief, holding back his wanting to laugh. After a few seconds with everyone staring up at the balloons caught in the tree, Nick's employer said, "I guess he's not ready to leave us yet."

The crying has stopped, but tears will still appear. There was a lot of crying in the beginning, of course, but I have heard of people who will not leave their house, sometimes not get out of bed, because they feel like they are going to cry in front of someone. Crying is a natural response to your grief. It is a release. I was never embarrassed about the tears I shed, because they were an integral part of my survival.

What do I do now, ten years later, to keep the memories alive? Writing has been my greatest outlet. This may sound strange, but whenever I sit down to write a story about Nick, I honestly feel he is standing next to me helping me to use the right words to express how I feel about everything that has happened. Journaling is a great way of expressing how you feel and getting those emotions down on paper. Many people say, "I can't write. I'm not a good writer." That's okay. You don't have to share your writing with anyone. In fact, if you do not want to hold on to that writing, just toss it in a wastepaper basket. The writing is for YOU, for your survival, for the happiness you deserve.

Friends and loved ones move on. They go back to their lives. When this happens, there can be a feeling of being left behind or being forgotten. This is another piece of the grieving process. My solution was to plan fun things to do, places to go, people to visit. My husband and I started taking mini vacations (my term for a long weekend) for a change of scenery and to be amongst people who did not know of our circumstances. We also enjoyed simply dropping into yard sales to see what bargains we could find.

I have continued to buy myself birthday presents from Nick. He was a renowned gift giver amongst his friends and family. A friend of his told me that Nick would agonize over what to get me for my birthday. I believe in paying it forward, so every year I keep my eyes open for something unique, something I would never buy for myself. When I find the perfect gift, I buy it and call it my birthday gift from Nick.

All in all, even though my life has been changed drastically, I decided to take positive steps, to climb with purpose over the rubble thrown in front of me. I stood strong when I heard the devastating news that Monday night, not even aware of how I was reacting. My belief now is that someone or something inspired me to stand and take charge, to move ahead with the strength that came from deep inside me.

I am intent on taking what I learned from Nick and paying it forward.

I want to help others move forward. As wonderful as hugs and kind words are, they won't provide ways to move ahead—but someone did provide me with all I needed, and that was Nick. He shared one of his class projects with me. It was brilliant. He purchased a beautiful wood carved box to create a memory box. I was so surprised when he showed me the contents. They were all items related to my father. I was so moved that he picked my dad for his project, a box of memories that you could open and admire at any given time.

I continue to receive messages from Nick. I call these messages gifts. Recently I was cleaning out a box of files that contained old paperwork that we were planning to shred. I told my husband that I had to quickly go through the files one more time before the shredding. While thumbing through the paperwork, the corner of a yellow lined paper stuck out of the top of one of the files. When I pulled it out, I pulled out three pages of a letter that started with, "Hey, it's me." I cried happy tears. It was a letter from Nick, about nothing. In fact, in the middle of the letter, he wrote, "Who the hell am I talking to? I make no sense. Why do I write like this? This is more like a talk-to-myself session here, and you're just listening in." I so miss Nick's sense of humor.

When I originally received the "Hey It's Me" letter, Nick hadn't written in a while. He was a busy sailor taking a few minutes to write to his mom about nothing. He knew I would appreciate it. I could picture him looking for the small yellow lined pad of paper that he used. He probably saw it and just absconded with it. I had a chance to visit his house in Hawaii where he was stationed. He lived with three other sailors. There was stuff everywhere. I think they were respectful of each other's rooms, but a pad of paper on the kitchen counter would have been free game.

I know in my heart that I was supposed to find that treasured piece of mail that day—a letter that was written years earlier. My emotions went from excitement to sadness to laughter. I was cleaning out these files in April; Nick had died in May five years earlier. I felt it was a sign—that he just wanted to say "hi," because it was "that time of year."

In summary, losing a child to suicide is devastating. Does it ever get easier? Will it get easier with time? No, it doesn't get easier, it just changes. Each year is different. Each holiday is different. I needed to learn how to take care of myself and how to have fun again. It is important that I accept that no one else is going to be able to guide me through this process of never-ending grief, and I do believe it is never ending but along with that comes personal growth. It is important to me, and it is important for me, to understand that others need to find their way in their own time. That is why I write about this topic.

People ask me what I want to accomplish with my writing, what is my goal? I will always answer, "If I can express a thought or share an idea that helps one person, that's my goal."

CHAPTER 3

The Year of Dad

In loving memory of James R. Wentz
August 17, 1934 to August 5, 2014

by Lisa Medley

I had chocolate chip pancakes and a cosmo. That was the most decadent meal I could think of after death. At a Long Island, New York diner at 11:00 p.m., this was my late dinner after witnessing my father take his last breath. I had just said goodbye to his body, one of the hardest acts in my life. After finishing packing up his possessions from the hospice facility and having an out-of-body conversation with the funeral home regarding his cremation, the open twenty-four-hours diner was the perfect place to nourish and numb.

I was accompanied by a dear friend that had just arrived from out-of-state. I had asked her to come a few days prior, knowing that the end was near. I gave myself permission to have support for the last leg of this journey. In the same moments my dad was leaving the planet, I felt my phone vibrating in my jeans pocket. She was texting me to say she had arrived at the nearby train station. She was right on time. As much as I am independent and strive for self-sufficiency, I knew in my bones that no one should ever do death or grief alone.

Reaching out for help was one of many strengths I developed over what I call "The Year of Dad." I experienced my dad's death and resulting grief in five phases: his heart surgery; hospice and death; my first summer of recovery; cleaning out his house; and my second summer of recovery. Now I am in the lifelong phase of living with grief. I have learned, and continue to learn, many life lessons of this inevitable and heartbreaking experience of being human. I invite you to read about this year of my life and perhaps be comforted by the personal and universal experience of grief.

The Year of Dad began the day before Father's Day in 2014. He called to inform me that he was in the hospital and scheduled to have triple-by-pass surgery in the next few days. I hung up the phone, almost hyperventilating, and packed a bag. The next day, I drove from my home state of Rhode Island to the Long Island, New York hospital and kept him company until his surgery. I had been planning to attend and present at a wellness conference that week. Given the fluctuations of hospital patient's needs, staff, and surgeons, I soon came to realize that I would either board the plane or I wouldn't. Priorities get crystal clear in these life situations. Fortunately, his surgery was scheduled in time for me to attend and more importantly, a success.

Unfortunately, his recovery was not. After a few days in the rehabilitation center where he was discharged, he was not doing well. Physically, he was making progress. Holistically, he was struggling. I had been home for a few days after my conference and began researching the rehabilitation process. I discovered that he could be placed closer to my home or my brother's home in Connecticut for more familial support. I drove to New York a few days before the July Fourth holiday to present him with this possibility. For a private man, I was pleasantly surprised that he was open, and grateful, for this option. We began the conversation and decided to make concrete plans the next day.

That next day didn't happen. I was staying over at his house and got a phone call at 4:00 a.m. from the rehabilitation center. They informed me that my dad was having trouble breathing and being transported back to the hospital where he received his surgery. It turned out that a nerve on the left side of his diaphragm muscle, essential for breathing, was not fully functioning. It was unclear if the nerve had been severed or was still in shock from the surgery. He spent the next week in the ICU and so did I.

My experience in the ICU was intense. I slept the first few nights in his room on a hospital recliner. There was a constant barrage of overstimulation from the lights, beeps, interrupted rest, and sounds of others suffering. Here we both were, experiencing trauma in different ways in a traumatic environment. It took me a few days to figure out that I didn't absolutely need to be there until doctors did their rounds first thing in the morning. I was in a foreign land without a translator. When I returned to his house for the night, it would take me hours to get the hospital sounds out of head.

As a holistic wellness professional, and my first experience in this kind of setting, I would often wonder, "Where is the healing?!" I appreciate the advances in medical technology and the people who have spent countless hours studying their profession and caring for patients. It is also clear that there is also a tremendous gap between life-or-death care and true healing that focuses on the whole person. I drew from my own toolbox and brought in a plant, made him a playlist of relaxation music, gave him an eye mask, and massaged his neck, shoulders, and hands.

After his physical body was stabilized, I believe he began to feel the emotional weight of his experience. He was treated for depression with medication, and we were told that this can sometimes happen after heart surgery. I thought to myself, "Are you kidding me? Sometimes? He just got his heart cut open!" His surgery preparation was all physical. He was informed about what was going to happen pre- and post-operation medically and encouraged to change his diet. That's it. There was no consultation for what he may experience emotionally or the mental tenacity it takes to recover.

A few weeks prior, when we were awaiting his surgery date, I told him that what was about to happen was a big deal. He said, "This is not a big deal, Lisa, people starving around the world is a big deal." I smiled gently. He cared for the world deeply, a value we share. I also knew that he had no idea what he was in for. My only major surgical experience, an unplanned C-Section for the birth of my son, took tremendous effort and many months to recover on every level of being. I was also caring for my newborn child, a feat in and of itself.

As an energy-sensitive person, it became clear to me many years ago that it was "embodiment or die." If I was going to thrive in this overstimulating world, I was not going to be able to sustain chronic survival mode or constant numbing. I also refused to settle for a mediocre life. To remedy this, I discovered (re-discovered) the value of my body's wisdom, personally and professionally. I expanded my body-centered toolbox and found ways to feel calmer, safe, and more centered. I also reclaimed my ability to feel vital, joyful, and free. I learned tools to quiet the intensity of the outer world and turn up the volume of my inner world. I honored my relationship with my body that included listening, trusting, and responding with kindness. When I followed my instincts and intuition, I felt more like myself. This is a daily practice that also has become my work in the world.

Understandably, my dad was not in touch with his body. He was taught like most humans to ignore most of what is happening from the neck down. This is an unfortunate result of ancient, warped programming for hundreds and thousands of years. He had a fairly to moderately healthy lifestyle and valued his intellect over everything else. The paradigm shift needed for him to experience his body in a new way was not going to happen overnight.

Over the next week on medication for his mental and emotional suffering, he became a hazy expression of himself. The drugs were dulling his otherwise sharp mental acuity. His existence was like watching suspended animation. I understand that it can take time for different medications to kick in and stabilize; however, this was a completely foreign experience for him and his body. The complications from surgery were unexpected. I felt just as overwhelmed in attempting to integrate a holistic approach in the context of the traditional medical model. I believe that the combination of this second experience in the hospital, the unknown healing path, and being forced to confront his body in such an intense way contributed to his final chapter.

I remember it like it was yesterday. After over a week in the ICU, I came into his room after a few errands during lunch. He looked at me with his sky-blue eyes. He told me he was done. He had completed what he wanted to do in his life with no regrets. I sobbed at his bedside. He told me it was okay to cry, giving me the space to do so. When I could breathe again, I could see his soul in his eyes. There was no doubt. I could feel a buoyancy, an energized relief, from his clarity of this decision. He was ready to leave this life behind. The healer in me kicked in. Through tears, I told him that I understood and would help make this transition as comfortable as possible. I stood firmly on the ground of sovereignty; his life was his and he got to choose how he lived, as well as how he died.

This declaration happened on a Friday. Even though the hospital was technically open all the time, it wasn't as much on the weekend. He was relocated to a different unit, and we were in limbo until Monday. During one of his naps that weekend, I finally looked at the pile of papers the hospital gives you when you arrive. In this pile was a brochure on palliative care. It talked about caring for the whole person. Imagine that.

I advocated for a visit from the palliative care team several times over the weekend. We finally received a visit on Monday morning. When one of the team members arrived, she sat on a stool next to my dad, eye level, and took his hand. She looked at him with kindness and listened deeply. When they were done talking, she knew what I knew to be true. He was ready to die. He was moved again to another unit, and we began the next step of locating a hospice facility.

This was not easy as he had to meet certain criteria. One hospice representative told us that his heart was functioning too well. I blinked at her with confusion. To help me understand, I reflected to her that even though he was suffering mentally and emotionally, the strength of his heart was at too high of a percentage to accept him. She confirmed that I was correct. I was stunned, though not surprised. After being in the holistic world for over twenty years, I am familiar with the limited perspectives to healing. However, this was my first experience to confront this reality in this way with my father's wellbeing at stake.

Finally, we connected with a hospice that adapted their checkboxes to fit our situation. Fortunately, it was also near the ocean on the coast of the Long Island Sound. The beach, the ocean waves, and the wooden boardwalk became a daily haven for me. I felt calmed by the people leisurely riding bicycles with plastic flowers on their baskets. Every day I could carve out a little slice of time to get away from my current weird reality of waiting for my father to die.

During this phase of The Year of Dad, I found my center by orientating around a brochure the hospice facility gave me. It had the signs of dying and a soft timeline that helped me track where he was in the process. I looked at it daily, sometimes multiple times. I held on to this brochure for dear life. I also had to remind myself to not get too attached to how his death was going to play out. This non-attachment practice became as stabilizing as the brochure. I strengthened my capacity to become really, really present.

During a game of chess, one of his favorites, I found myself wondering if this was going to be the last game we play together. I heard my inner wisdom draw me back to the moment and say, "Be in the game." Other times, I would flounder. Do I stay or do I go? I wanted to be with him as much as possible. I also needed to eat or get a break from the place where people are dying in every room. Sacrificing my basic needs and not giving myself the occasional break in this process was not going to help anyone. What sometimes felt like my-life-or-his-death dilemma became a stronger stand in self-care reclamation.

I knew my dad would want that for me. When he was in the hospital for the second time, he told me that I had better take care of myself. He saw me as the middle of his wheel with the spokes being talking to his various doctors, navigating his care, and managing his external life. I confidently said, "I got this." I assured him that I knew how to take care of myself. I was doing all I could to stay mentally sharp and energetically astute. Even though I was already in anticipatory grief, sleep deprived, and running on adrenaline, I also knew that this experience was time limited. Most of the time, I ate nutritious food, drank plenty of water, walked on the beach, and talked with my family and friends. I would relish playing pretend that nothing bad was happening in my life while looking at dishes or shoes or anything mundane in nearby department stores. Although his inevitable death was always just below the surface, I would float above this reality from time to time to preserve my sanity.

My dad died on the thirty-sixth day of what I thought was going to be a thirty-six-hour visit back in late June. It was the day after my son's birthday. Although I had drove home a few days prior to attend a party we had scheduled for my son and his friends, I was in New York on his actual birthday. Before going to visit my dad at the hospice facility that morning, I called my husband and son to hear about the birthday celebration. After hearing about the special day, I told my husband that I woke up feeling strange, like I only wanted to watch movies all day. It was such an odd experience to feel the urge to do that with the knowledge that my dad was literally on this deathbed. When I arrived at the hospice facility,

I learned that he had lost consciousness overnight. It seems that I had felt like "checking out" because he was doing the same. The hospice staff confirmed that he was in the final stages of his life. His death would likely occur within the next twenty-four hours.

After the staff left his room and I was alone with him, I got out of small bundle of sage from a drawer. I had been guided by my intuition to get some a week before. It was time. I lit it lightly to not set off the sprinklers. I moved it around the room and found myself focusing on the top of his head, I believe to clear the channel above. Even though I know I was doing this, it felt like this action was being done through me. It even felt familiar, like I had done this before, though not in this lifetime.

This was the first day in thirty-five days that I didn't have any response from him as to what would be most helpful. There was no more eye contact, no more head nods, no more hand squeezing. All I had left to track was his breathing until his last one. This day became a deeper practice of trust, love, and surrender. There was nothing more I could do but be. It was a preview of the most difficult letting go that would come that night.

I had with me a journal which I wrote in that afternoon at his bedside. One of my last entries before he died reads:

> "Now at the end, I don't have any feedback, so I ebb and flow out of letting him know that I'm here, taking care of myself and letting him have some space. I don't know anymore if my presence is helpful to him or not, so I trust my instincts—listen to my heart, follow my body's needs for food, fresh air, water, a call to a friend. He would want me to continue to take care of myself, so I wave in and out of presence and spaciousness for him and me."

A few weeks prior, when it was clear that his death would come sooner than later, I experienced a knowing that I was supposed to be there when he died. I also heard from many people that sometimes the dying person wants to be alone and waits until their loved ones leave the room. I felt confused after that, not wanting to hold him back from his timing nor impose what may be my agenda. On the day he lost consciousness, I had no way of knowing if he knew I was there. However, I was told that hearing was the last of the senses to go. Throughout that day, I decided to tell him when I left the room and for how long, so he could be given the space needed to die.

As it turned out, I was in the room. When he took his last breath, his whole body contracted into itself, like the fetal position of newborn. His body was returning to its original shape. Then it was still. A peaceful, haunting quiet. I nodded to my inner knowing in affirmation that I was indeed meant to witness his final moment of life and be initiated into this moment of death.

Anticipatory grief was over. Living with grief had begun. As the hospice facility staff did what they needed to do for him, I stepped into the hallway to make travel arrangements for my friend who had just arrived at the train station to be brought to me. I called my brother who was awaiting the news nearby. When he arrived, we sat on a bench outside for a long time in silence. I gave him my dad's watch.

My friend arrived at the facility soon after and held me as I collapsed in tears. Although I was alone with my dad's death, I was supported during the first waves of grief. She stayed with me as I called the funeral home. I have no idea what I said but was assured that they would take care of him. She waited in the lobby while I said my final goodbye to his body, an excruciating act. I collected his things and clutched the clock that we had brought from his house as I departed the room for the last time. When I was ready to leave the building, my friend took the car keys and drove us to that Long Island diner where I ate breakfast and drank cocktails until the middle of the night.

Going to sleep that night was almost unbearable. The activity of the day was over, and grief was beginning. I cried myself to sleep. I woke up crying. It was like an icy wind of awareness, biting at my heart over and over and over as I began to face what had just happened. Even though I knew he died, I was also disorientated and in disbelief. It was like my brain could not fully compute all at once. I suspect this mechanism exists in us humans to help us digest the experience of loss in smaller bites, otherwise we might not make it through.

The next few days were an emotional whirlwind of making phone calls, napping when I could, and staring into space. My friend was with me, ensuring I was eating, introducing me to a new sitcom for a mental break, and helping me with tasks. One of those was going to the funeral home to make the final arrangements for his cremation. I felt like I was moving through mud. As we slowly walked up to the front door, she paused and reminded me that I only had to do this once. Those wise words helped me go inside and make the choices I need to make.

Almost a week after his death, I finally drove home to Rhode Island. When I pulled my car in the driveway, my son came outside to give me the biggest and best hug in the world. I carried him, my heavy heart, weary body, and exhausted mind inside. I was relieved to be home. I also knew that The Year of Dad was far from over. Not only did we need to plan for his memorial service, but his house also needed to be taken care of, a mammoth task. Before I took on that project, I gave myself the rest of the summer to recover.

It was mid-August now. I took on the responsibility of driving my son to and from camp for a few weeks. After camp drop off, I drove to the water. A benefit of living in Rhode Island, the Ocean State, is that there is a plethora of beaches to visit. I would sit for hours, looking at the waves a few hundred miles of coastline north of where I last saw my dad. I couldn't get enough of the sound of waves. It was incredibly soothing for my frayed nerves. Those were the only actions I did for the rest of the summer. My son and self-care were the priority. My husband, a rock-star of a single dad all summer, also had a reprieve from full on parenting. I am very fortunate that he was a hands-on dad. His love and care for our son contributed immensely to my ability to be a devoted caregiver to my dad all those weeks.

My dad's death didn't end the day he died. At the end of the summer, with my son back in school, I began to turn towards the material remains of his life. When I was with my dad in his final weeks, I was only focused on him. I was completely unprepared for the number of tasks and details I would need to tend to after he died. Each item was a trigger for grief that ranged in intensity.

One of those items was the delivery of his ashes in a box from the New York funeral home. This brought me to my knees, literally. I cannot recall the exact circumstances, but for some reason his ashes needed to be mailed to me. When the post office person knocked on the door for me to sign for this package, it was all I could do to stay standing. After I closed the door, I set the heavy box down in the hallway and ran into the kitchen where I crumpled into a heap on the floor sobbing. It was like he had died all over again. I called my husband, still at work, and then a friend who was able to come over. When she arrived, I was still on the floor. We eventually walked outside to our porch and sat with me for a few hours until I could get my emotional footing again.

Then the medical bills started to arrive in the mail. I would pour myself a glass of wine, sometimes two, and pay them. I would try to pretend that they were just pieces of paper instead of reminders of the last weeks of my dad's life. I had all his mail forwarded to me, so every time something arrived, I would receive yet another item to close out. I asked my husband to help with some of them and cancelled or unsubscribed anything I could online. I still needed to speak with all his financial institutions and other providers that he no longer had needs for like his dentist. Every one of these conversations activated the pain in my already heavy heart.

Then there was his house. This began the next phase of The Year of Dad. I lived in this house from ages seven to fourteen. We moved there from upstate New York after he became the minister for the local Unitarian Universalist congregation. I moved away when I was fourteen after my parents' divorce. Since it had been a few decades from when I left, I was not attached to the house. However, my dad was. A child of the depression era, my dad learned to be resourceful and keep everything in case you might need it. Although he was not a hoarder, he was not a throwaway-er. Cleaning out the three-thousand-square-foot house that also had an attic, basement, and a garage full of belongings became my life for what became the next nine months.

My dad had left the house to me and my brother. It was a gift we were deeply grateful for. It was also one that needed a tremendous amount of attention before receiving. Neither of us were going to live there, so prepping it for sale was the next course of action. The taxes were astronomical, so selling it had to be done as fast as possible. I also wanted to get back to my life. So began my commute between Rhode Island and New York about every other weekend from a few days to a week.

I remember standing in the living room on my first house cleaning trip in September, about a month after he died. I felt the weight of what I was about to embark on. I looked around at all the rooms filled with the stuff of his life in a daze. After what felt like hours, my mind cleared, and like the last puzzle piece being put into place, I began to accept that the house was not going to clean itself. It was up to me to make this happen. As a friend of mine wisely shared, "There is no estate fairy," a truth that she, too, had to contend with when she cleaned out her parents' house many years prior.

I cannot express in words this monumental task. It often felt like it would never end. There was so much stuff. I continued my self-care to the best of my ability so I could have the energy required. I listened to music daily and sang at the top of my lungs, both essential and medicinal for my soul. I continued to eat well, though I did add a steady diet of wine to my menu. I would drive to natural settings and walk. I would escape in mindless television, late-night movies, and anything that did not require too much thought. I would call friends to keep me company as I sorted out desk drawers and endless boxes of papers.

I did all of this while I was fresh in grief. I would cry at the most random times. Sometimes I would stop what I was doing, feel, and then move on or take a nap. Other times I would ignore the impulse and push through. The times I was able to be present with my emotions, I would experience them as an ocean wave. Sometimes the wave would knock me over, sometimes it was like a ripple at my ankles. When I allowed the full emotional wave to move through me, I strengthened my trust that this feeling would indeed pass. Even though at times it felt like I would shatter into a million pieces, I didn't. There were also times that I just couldn't feel anymore and would numb out or space out. I allowed myself those times too. One of my dad's phrases growing up was, "Just do the best you can, Lisa." So, I did.

Early on in this process, I reflected if I should get a dumpster and just toss everything, but I didn't for two reasons. One, I saw that for every item I picked up a decision needed to be made: keep, toss, donate. I decided that if that item could be utilized by someone else, I would rather pass it on than put it in the trash. A little more effort though a lot less waste. At an early age, my parents taught me the importance of recycling and reusing. This was decades before it was "popular." Being thoughtful of how to release the contents of his house was a way to honor him. He would want me to do it this way. I also care deeply about the Earth, so this mindful process was aligned with my values.

The second reason was that every now and then I would find treasures like this journal entry he wrote on the day I was born.

"Much has occurred since the last entry—reading and preparing and delivering sermons; planning the total re-plumbing of all water lines from tanks. But tonight's entry is significant and most exciting for at 7:36 p.m., Lisa Ann Wentz was born. Words do not convey our happiness upon her arrival—our first child. She comes into a very troubled world, but she will bring it her spirit of peace and common sense."

I would have missed this heartfelt thread that wove my life with his if it had been thrown away.

There were other precious items as well. I came across a small wooden unicorn from my childhood collection. I discovered the hard copies of his sermons that I will scan for posterity one day. Towards the end of cleaning out the attic, I found two five-drawer file cabinets with folders from all the people he performed wedding ceremonies for over the years. This was his main profession after he retired from ministry, so there were hundreds. Each folder contained personal information, including social security numbers. I placed every one of them into boxes and drove them to a local shredding facility. I personally watched them be cut into teeny tiny pieces. I know my dad would have done the same thing.

I did receive help periodically from a few friends as well as my brother throughout these nine months. Since I was a few states away from my family and friends, and my husband had his hands full with our son, it was not as easy to have ongoing help than if he had lived nearby. This aspect of his material life could have been easier and not have taken so long if some clearing out had been done while he was still alive. However, he was a private person, and I imagine it never occurred to him the toll it would take on me and my life. I had not thought about it either. I now know that this is one of many aspects that needs to be tended to after losing a loved one.

One day when I was home in Rhode Island, my son asked me if I was going to move to New York. Ouch. He had a six-year-old understanding that Grandpa was not "living on the Earth" anymore. He also was experiencing my continued absence. Even though I explained the best I could of what I needed to do, I also felt the emotional stretch as a mother that needs to be in too many places at once.

In the eighth month, the house was ready to be put on the market. My brother and I sought a cash buyer since the house needed a great deal of work. My mantra during this time was, "I release this house with ease and grace," since the pool of potential buyers was smaller. After some tense weeks, we found one. The last of the donations were delivered, the final clean up began, and papers were signed. I could finally go home and resume my life of the living.

The check for the house came in the mail early June, almost a full year after I received that first phone call from my dad the previous June. The final phase of The Year of Dad began as I used the rest of that summer to recover, again. I felt brittle and strong, empty and full, heartbroken and inspired all at the same time. I had witnessed one of the most painful moments in life, initiated into the tribe of daughters and sons who lose a parent. I began my journey of living with grief.

Even though I had been grieving while cleaning out his house, I put a temporary hold on most of the healing process so I could keep focusing on the task at hand. There was no way I was going to be able to fully process what I had been through and deconstruct my dad's material life simultaneously. The house had become my life. It was only now, a year later, that I could face the loss while integrating myself back into my life.

Most of the time I felt heavy, sad, and in a haze. I often felt like the character Eeyore from Winnie the Pooh, plodding through my life, my heart drooping. I would stare off into space and forget what I was doing. I had no idea when I would tear up or downright weep at nothing in particular. It was unnerving and felt like the ground under my feet kept shifting. I lived through the lens of loss; it was almost all that I could see.

When I was around another person and felt sad or started crying unexpectedly, what helped the most was someone just being with me and my feelings. Especially in the moments of heartbreak, phrases like "at least he had a good life" or "he is no longer suffering" did not comfort me. I just wanted to cry. Depending on the person, sometimes I could be supported in the way that I needed, other times not. Feeling sad and then disappointed on top of it because someone was wanting to "make it better" made me feel hollow inside. I learned, and continue to learn, that if someone is not able to be present for my feelings, it may because they have not been supported to feel in this way themselves. When I remember, I choose wisely who I share my grief with.

Sometimes the emotional disconnect is from the lack of knowing of what to do or say. I don't always know either! This is not uncommon. The reality is that our culture does not do grief well, nor much of the human experience of feeling, sensing, and being. The value has been placed on the activities of thinking and doing for hundreds and thousands of years. Navigating the inner landscape can be challenging for the one who is feeling as well as for those witnessing. I don't want to see anyone in pain and have my moments of wanting to "fix." When I can remember to be still and allow someone to have their experience, even the painful ones, that is the healing. When I am courageous enough to say what I need or ask another who is in pain what they need, that is also powerful.

Critical to soothing my emotional self was restoring my physical self. As an energetically sensitive person and a holistic wellness professional, I knew that I needed to give myself extra time and space to return to some sense of balance. My body didn't know that what I had been doing for the last year was for my dad; all it knew was utter exhaustion. I knew that if I didn't give myself more time being and less time doing, the year-long physiological and energetic survival mode would catch up with me and potentially catalyze more dis-ease. I had already been through enough. Burnout, go-go-go, and crash-and-burn are unhealthy rhythms I am familiar with. Over the years, I have learned to adjust my lifestyle to minimize that experience. I am a better version of myself when I pace myself. I now trust the process of restoration.

One of the best ways I restored, and still do, is sleep. During that second summer of recovery, it was not always restful sleep. I was still feeling the energetic aftershocks of my previous year intensely. I also couldn't get the duration of sleep I really needed as a mom. I did my best to balance my needs with my son's; the lifelong, challenging journey of motherhood. If it wasn't extra sleep, it was at least a slower pace and minimal items on my to-do list. When I was able to sleep as much as what my body needed, I could feel the positive impact on my wellbeing.

In addition to sleep, I added in other healing modalities. One of the restful practices already in my self-care toolbox is Yoga Nidra. This is a type of yoga where the only pose is stillness while you are guided to bring awareness to different parts of your body. This type of body scan is powerfully restorative for the body and brain. I began to receive massage therapy periodically again and started acupuncture which offered me a new experience of deep relaxation. To feel stronger and more grounded, I started personal training at my local YMCA which helped me to access a quality of warrior-like strength I had not fully tapped into. Spending time in nature was, and still is, essential. Wide open spaces, ocean waves, and a quiet forest helps me to slow down and just be. I can more easily hear myself think, tap into feelings I may be ignoring, and sometimes receive insight and guidance.

Engaging in these practices were not a luxury. I knew I needed a multidimensional approach to put myself back together. I didn't know how long it was going to take for me to feel better, and I trusted the process. I remember a weekend in mid-August of this second summer of recovery where I slept almost twelve hours both Saturday and Sunday. The following week, I finally felt more like myself. My nervous system had received the kind of rest it needed. I felt like my energy tank was more full than empty. The combination of sleep, healing modalities, and less to-do's helped me turn a corner in my healing process. These are restorative ways that worked for me. Everybody needs something different at different times.

As I restored my body, I also resumed regular family life. My son, almost seven, and I spent uninterrupted quality time playing and enjoying summertime activities. Fortunately, he was resilient, adventurous, and lived in the present most of the time. After experiencing death, I found myself saying "yes" to many of life's little joys, like getting ice cream sprinkles shaped like dinosaurs! This was one of my son's passions and I can still remember the lightness in my heart, a welcome relief, when we found them in the baking aisle of a local grocery store.

My husband and I have been married almost twenty-two years. He is a kind, generous, and loving man, husband, and father. When I finished my master's thesis many years ago, my dedication to him was, "…to the eye of my hurricane." He is a calm center when I at times am spinning too fast. Since we have been together so long, he knows of my sensitive nature and that I need extra rest and downtime in general, never mind this current experience. As long as I let him know what I need for survival and sanity, he is supportive and says, "Do what you need to do." I like the version of myself that is more rested, patient, and kind. He does too. Throughout the summer, we were able to find our life rhythm again and he now had more time to catch up with himself after being a part-time single parent for most of a year.

In addition to restoration and connecting with my family life, the only specific task I gave myself that summer was to organize my jewelry drawer, only if I felt like it. This was for the part of me that wanted to feel accomplished by "doing" something. It was achievable, playful, and pressure-free. I needed to keep the to-do's very simple and short since I couldn't focus for very long. My brain was fatigued with the toll grief takes and the thousands of decisions I made while clearing out my dad's house. The smaller the items on my to-do list, or in shorter time increments, the better. This way, when I would find myself staring off into space, I wouldn't be so hard on myself.

Most of my work is creative and requires deep presence to projects and people. I couldn't give what I didn't have. I would vacillate between feeling impatient and compassionate with myself and knew that I couldn't do too much at once. I did discover that when I eased the pressure off to "make something happen" and allowed myself a wide mental berth, often ideas would emerge naturally. Even when I wasn't producing anything, I could trust that the inner voice of inspiration was still there. By the end of the summer, I was able to return to most of my vocational life and begin creating, learning, and growing again. This was another confirmation of trusting the restoration process. With time, space, and healing choices, my inner well did get filled again and I was able to participate in my life again more fully.

Feeling and healing my grief did not stop at the end of this summer. Although I was reestablishing rhythms of my life, my heart was still tender, though not quite as raw. Instead of feeling the chronic hum of sadness, there were longer moments of just living life. The feelings of grief would still come and go, though they wouldn't stay as long or grip as tight.

What I had not anticipated was what I now call the "firsts"—his first birthday, first holiday, and the first Father's Day without him. Also, the first anniversary of his death. The first birthday occurred twelve days after he died. I honestly don't remember that day. I was away on a previously planned vacation week with my family and at that point, the days were hazy and mushed together. It came and went and got lost in the shuffle of my already deep sadness.

Thanksgiving was the first holiday that I was acutely aware of his lack of presence. We hosted this holiday, his idea almost twenty years ago. He had pointed out that we were the geographical epicenter of our respective families. After everyone had arrived except him, I felt a wave of grief course through me. I became painfully aware of yet another reminder that he was no longer alive. Christmas was a little less intense since we celebrated with different family members each year and didn't have as many annual traditions. The first Father's Day, I cried in the department store aisle picking out a card for my husband and not my dad. My dad really didn't care about cards, though I sent him one every year anyway.

The first anniversary of his death was difficult. All I knew was that I wanted to be at the beach, held by the sand and sea. Since I was present when he died, I also knew the minute of his passing. I was in the car when that moment came as my husband drove my son and I to the beach. I was watching the clock and when that exact minute came, I held onto the passenger door handle for dear life and breathed. I had survived the first year.

For the holidays, birthdays, and death anniversaries that have come since, the anticipation of the pain has sometimes been worse than the actual experience. However, I have learned to proactively plan for spaciousness, especially for the anniversary of his death. What that means to me is little to no to-do's that day. I do not know what state of being I will be in and will have just celebrated my son's birthday the previous day. Sometimes the memories and corresponding grief are a passing pull on my heart. Other times it knocks me over.

The year my son turned ten brought me to a new awareness of grief. I was experiencing an intense blend of joy, sadness, and relief about my son turning double digits. The following day was the four-year anniversary of my dad's death, and I felt like he had just died all over again. I was caught off guard by how time seemed to collapse. I called my friend who had been with me the day he died and sobbed. Fortunately, she is an excellent listener, didn't judge the timeline, and could hold the space for me to feel the depth of pain that I was not prepared for.

This experience taught me two more important lessons. The first one was the relationship between grief and time. Life is not linear, neither is grief. I realized that perspectives such as "get over it" or any timeline driven expectations are warped reflections from our disconnected culture. The pressure to feel a certain way by a certain time is too much to ask of anyone, especially when you are grieving. That is not human and certainly not humane. There is no right way, nor is there is "normal" to return to. When you lose someone, so-called normal no longer exists. All anyone can really do is one day at a time, sometimes just one moment or even a breath at a time.

The second lesson was learning to give grief the respect it deserves. It is a distinct entity on the emotional scale of human experience. I have come to know grief like a wild animal, coming and going as it pleases. I never know when it decides to arrive and how long it will stay. I suffer less when I bow down to its presence, soften my resistance, and feel whatever is present. This is easier said than done. I do my best to tend to this emotional visitor until the weight lifts and the air clears when it leaves.

Grief is personal and universal. Right after he died, I felt like I was the only person who had ever experienced the loss of a loved one. The intensity of emotions would sometimes shroud my ability to remember that I was not alone. When I did share my experience with my friends who had lost one or both parents, and even children, I found great comfort. I didn't even know that I needed this kind of social medicine, especially when I was in my "I'm the only one who has ever gone through this" moment. Just like any experience in life, when you relate with someone who has been through what you have, there is an unspoken understanding. I didn't have to explain all of what I was thinking or feeling. I likely couldn't have if I tried. There is relief in that.

An example of this kind of support occurred shortly before I was to scatter my dad's ashes with some family members. A woman from my dad's hospice organization spontaneously called me a few days before this event to check in. I shared that I was feeling untethered about this upcoming event, my first time doing this experience. She told me about when she released her dad's ashes with her siblings. She said there had been a plan as to where and when, but the part of who and how had not yet been established. She explained that when the time came to actually do the scattering, she and her family looked around at each other in confusion as to what to do next. They muddled through this moment with humor, awkwardness, and honor at the same time. This helped to ground me as I prepared to encounter this difficult and sacred experience.

The most powerful moment of the universal human connection was when my dad was in the hospital between post-surgery complications and hospice. One of those long days, I was walking down the hallway on my way to the chapel. I would sometimes lie down in a pew and rest in quiet. I remember stopping mid step and saw in front of me a lobby full of other humans keeping watch for their loved ones. They may have been waiting for death, birth, surgery, recovery, or discharge. In that moment, it didn't matter. What I felt was the interconnected nature of humanity. We really are all in this life together and no one should, or needs to, do these kind of life experiences alone.

As the eldest with high achieving tendencies, I am well versed, and take a certain amount of pride, in my ability to do things on my own. Navigating this Year of Dad humbled me to a saner balance of being independent and asking for help. Aside from loving my dad, I was out of my comfort zone almost all the time. There were so many aspects about this phase in my life that I had never done. I was forced to confront my reluctance to ask for help. As I allowed myself to be in the not knowing most of the time, I found myself supported in ways that I was not accustomed. I remember thinking, "This is so much easier!" When I was pregnant with my son, I received advice from a wise person who said, "When anyone offers to help, say yes." Little did I know that this was true on the other end of the life cycle as well. Nowadays, sometimes I remember to ask for help, sometimes I forget. However, I wouldn't have learned to let myself off the rugged-individual hook without this experience.

In addition to softening my vulnerability to receive support, I also learned to grant myself more grace with the emotional journey of grief. It can be messy. Sometimes it is like a tangled ball of yarn that tugs on other unhealed losses, disappointments, and regrets that still reside within. Even within the grief experience itself, there can be a confusing range of emotions from sadness and relief to anger and gratitude. Remember Sally Field in the post funeral scene in "Steel Magnolias"? Your emotions are your experience, and you get to feel them all.

You have likely heard "time heals all wounds." I agree, though with a caveat: to heal, you must feel. I understand the desire to not want to feel the depth of pain that grief brings. I would never voluntarily sign up for this at times excruciating experience. Even though I know intellectually that feeling is necessary, when the pain is present, the survival instinct to resist the heartbreak puts up a fight. However, it cannot be bypassed. The energy of grief, and every emotion, needs to move. If it doesn't, it will get stuck and take up residence in the body, negatively impacting your wellbeing. I have cried through many paragraphs of this chapter. I have also resisted to feel the pain along the way. However, I must dive into the emotional wave and write myself through to the other side. Then, I see again that I am still in one piece.

You don't have to feel your emotions in isolation. Sometimes I need a good cry by myself. Other times, I have called on support to process painful experiences that I won't willingly enter by myself. I need a trusted guide in a safe container so I can unwind the inner contraction, even a little. Sometimes this is a friend, other times it is a mentor or therapeutic professional. Give yourself the gift of support, tools, and modalities for all the dimensions of who you are. As you experience more lightness of being, you get to express more of the true you.

In hindsight, I would have done a few things differently. I'm not beating myself up or regretful; I didn't know what I didn't know. I share these in the spirit of what I learned, what I will consider for the future, and what may help you on your path.

I would have reached out for even more support. Especially in the moments where I felt all alone or victimized by the experience. I would have given myself more time to just be and feel while I was cleaning out his house. I would have taken a day or more off to do nothing or whatever I felt like it. I usually had this inner pressure to get it done as fast as possible. A few days here and there would not have made a huge difference. I would have created an alter with my dad's picture and meaningful items and a candle. After he died, I couldn't, or wouldn't, look at his picture for years. It hurt too much. I see now that my resistance to the pain also blocked the appreciation of what I did receive from him. Although I wasn't completely unaware of what he taught me, I now know that my heart would have had more of a chance to fill while it was feeling empty.

I also would have been more insistent, with love, to address his house and the contents within it. Since it was my first experience with this type of cleaning out, I had no idea what it would take and the impact it had on my life. For those of you who have family in their elder years and have not yet discussed this physical reality after they have gone, consider a conversation or at least put it on your radar. Depending on the person and circumstances, action may or may not be able to occur. The reality is that your loved one's "stuff" is part of the grief process.

An aspect of the estate process that my dad handled with gusto was getting all his paperwork in order. Shortly after my husband's mother passed away many years ago, I was introduced to the world of losing a parent. After that, I bravely opened the door to the end-of-life conversation. I remember taking a deep breath and asking him if he had anything in place. He said he had nothing. A few months later, he had everything. He invested in an estate lawyer and gave my brother and I copies of all the documents. He also included all his financial information, passwords, ideas of where to donate his body, and location request of where to scatter his ashes. My dad was a detail orientated man and for this, especially in this area of his life, I am deeply grateful.

Talking about death, paperwork, and last wishes is not easy. However, it is worthwhile. As soon as my dad handed me the folder with everything I would need, I put it in my home safe. When I made the first visit to the New York hospital, as well as my second, I carried it around. It gave me confidence that even if there was a point he couldn't communicate, I knew his wishes. The information made many of the logistics of closing his material life easier. I felt appreciative that these details were literally at my fingertips during an already difficult time. It is one of those conversations that as soon as you cross the threshold to having it, the result will eventually give you peace of mind.

I am closing this chapter with a deeper understanding of grief. It continues to show up in my life, solid and fluid at the same time. It has its own presence, with palpable depth, weight, and mass. When it is there, I know it. Grief is also like an amoeba, changing form as it moves throughout my life. It has changed how much space it takes up over time. During the anticipatory grief phase in hospice and in that first year, grief was in the foreground. Now almost seven years later, it has receded to the background most of the time.

However, grief continues to surprise me. A month ago, I was in a home improvement store getting copies of keys made. The gentleman who helped me was about my dad's age, with a similar build and kind eyes. While he placed the keys in the machine, I found myself silently weeping. This time though it was comforting. I felt like I was with him. Every time my dad came to visit, usually a couple of times a year, we always went to this store at least twice. He was very handy and helped with house projects during his visit. Upon leaving the store, I realized that I could come to this store for a "dad fix" and visit with this familiar energy. I felt uplifted by his memory, a new experience for me. The sadness had become so familiar that I didn't know there was another way to feel. The lightness in my heart was hopeful and added another dimension to the complex experience of grief.

Losing a loved one is never over; it becomes part of the fabric of life. Although each experience is unique, it is shared with every human on the planet at some point. Confronting death and living with grief is one of the most difficult parts of being human. Shortly after my dad's death, one of my friends whose parents are still alive said, "I can't imagine what you are going through." I paused, reflected, and then found myself saying, "You are not supposed to." It was a realization that there are some moments in life we are not meant to experience until we do. I continue to practice giving grief respect for the shape shifter it is. When it shows up, I call on one of my dad's gifts, "Do the best you can." I do and so will you.

CHAPTER 4

But We Were Going to be Bitchy Old Ladies Together...

In loving memory of the loss of all best friends...

by Elizabeth Phinney

"I'll let you know when I get back—I'll give you a call."

"Okay," was her reply. "Love you!"

"Love you back," I answered. And that was it. Our last phone call, our last conversation, our last live connection.

I was in Florida that February, basking in the sunshine, just weeks before the pandemic that continues to change our lives struck. I was taking a walk and thought I would give my best bud a call to see how she was doing with her multitude of projects. We blathered on for about ten minutes. In hindsight I wish it had been hours.

It was a Thursday, and I was flying home that Sunday. She was heading to New Hampshire to visit a friend and take in some beautiful snow activities. It took me a few days after getting home before I ventured down the rabbit hole of Facebook. After a minute or two of scrolling, I kept seeing "RIP Elaine," "I'll miss you so much, Elaine," "RIP Elaine Semper. You will be missed."

I thought, *how weird*. So, I picked up the phone and called her: "You won't believe this. There's a whole bunch of people on Facebook saying you died. That is so weird. Call me!"

As I continued to scroll and saw more and more postings, I ran downstairs with my phone and handed it to my daughter. "It says Elaine died... Did she die?"

After about thirty agonizing seconds, she slowly looked up and said, "Yeah, Mom. She did."

I felt like I had been hit by a truck, right in the center of my chest. In a zombie-like fog, I crawled back up to my room and sat down on the bed. This was beyond comprehension. She was only sixty-one years old. She wasn't sick. She had nothing wrong with her. I knew because we shared this stuff together. We shared pretty much everything. I kept scrolling through Facebook, desperate to find that this was all a mistake. That it was a cruel joke.

I'm not sure how long I sat on my bed. I do remember having to stand up, though, because my back and neck were hurting from spending so much time on my phone in that crouched over position. I felt so empty. Endlessly scrolling and hoping. I found it was a highly effective way to stall melting into a puddle of tears—you can't read well when you are crying, so I kept scrolling.

How would it be that I could never speak to her again? Elaine was my business coach and had helped me map out all the ups and downs of my business and where I was taking it. She tolerated my procrastination and my jumping around with goals and directions and priorities WITHOUT JUDGMENT. Who does that? But she did. She knew how to talk to me and calm me down and not get defensive. Her ideas were always good, and though we didn't necessarily agree with the approach I should take all the time, we could then agree to disagree. She was my biggest fan and believed in me and boosted my spirits when I needed it.

We had also become best friends, that kind of friend who gets you, who you don't have to explain things to or who asks all the right questions. Who knows when not to pry. The kind with whom you can share space and not say a word, or say one line and you both are in hysterics, laughing harder than you knew you could.

She had her fair share of issues going on, too, I must say. Some pretty rough family situations that she really didn't tell anyone but me. She felt comfortable enough with me to pretty much share it all, from childhood to marriage to adoption to divorce to siblings to parents—a life filled with good stuff, but some pretty heart-wrenching relationships. I felt honored that she trusted me with her darkest secrets. Needless to say, I was equally an open book with her. But, neither one of us dwelled on the heartache we had every right to feel based on our life history. We agreed to be positive and hopeful, uplifting and light-hearted, grateful and more grateful.

To get you on the same page as to where I was when this happened, my life at the time was at a turning point. I had been a single mom of three children for over twenty years and my career during the last fifteen of those challenging years was as a personal trainer. But even before I chose that as a profession, I knew that I was destined to be a teacher—to share information that I knew with people who wanted to know what I knew. I had done that in a previous career, and it felt so right. Once I found fitness as my new path, I knew it was just a matter of time before I would be ready to share my knowledge.

I had been working one on one with men and women, my forte being Fitness After Forty Five™. I was also teaching classes in a meditative strength training technique I have created called BodSpir®. Business was quite good, but I knew that I needed to do some things differently to get myself to the next level. But then, in 2009, my son was killed—he was twenty-one. (There are a few women in this book who are sharing their stories about losing a child, giving some insights into that heart wrenching, but empowering, life experience.) That following year was a wash, needless to say, but after that year of mourning was over, I sensed my son's presence as he told me to get going—I had had my year. It was time for me to start making some changes to my career and expand the wisdom I had learned as a personal trainer.

Knowing I was about to launch a new business, I realized I was pretty uninformed about how to do that in the new millennium. I was confident in my ability as I had had my own successful business in my pre-kids career, but that was in the '80s. Things had changed. So, as I followed sign after sign, I was guided to a multitude of guru's involved in all aspects of business and marketing and social media and video making and speaking. Beginning November 2011 in Santa Clara, California and ending in Phoenix, Arizona in June 2014, I attended fourteen conferences and traveled all over the country. What an amazing journey I had taken and a plethora of professionals I met, many of whom I now call friends.

When I returned home and settled in, I started to look for a local women's networking group. I found one where the speaker was so much like so many of the professionals I had met, I had to meet her. I ended up hiring her coaching services to start to get a plan together and see what track I should take as I moved forward. It was through her encouraging words for me to network and meet folks from around my home state that took me on a whirlwind of networking events for the next five years around Rhode Island and nearby Massachusetts, and soon led me to meet my new best friend!

The Universe works in mysterious ways, in case you hadn't noticed this by now. I was at a networking event hosted by none other than Susan Lataille, who spearheaded this collaborative book. I asked her a question and she directed me down the hall to a potential speaking venue that I might like. I met the manager of the venue and she introduced me to the publisher of a local magazine, who I happened to be writing a letter to that was sitting on my computer screen—talk about your small world! Anyway, they were both starting in a mastermind group at the end of the week and asked if I would be interested. I, of course, accepted. It was to be on Friday, May 1, 2015.

It was a small group—I think there were eight of us, all women. One of the women was a business coach, Elaine Semper (her name has been changed for privacy). She seemed very bright, great sense of humor and very articulate in her knowledge. We chatted briefly after the meeting and exchanged contact information. I told her I might be interested in hiring her services and discovered we lived about forty-five minutes apart. A few weeks later, we arranged to meet and take a look at what I was doing and how she might be able to help.

That first meeting that Elaine and I had was in a coffee shop in her hometown. I brought some files and ideas with me and so did she—all for naught! We sat in that shop for three hours just chatting it up. I think we touched on business a little, but, for each of us, it was mainly creating a connection with a woman who you clicked with in so many ways. We told scattered stories of our lives and recognized that we each had had our fair share of trauma. We were both moving on from our pasts and were thrilled to make a new friend with whom to explore new opportunities.

After that meeting, we spent lots of time on the phone and conferring on business ideas—marketing was her thing, so it was fabulous to get so many other insights and ideas on promoting my business. If I was doing a trade show, she would not only help me set up the booth but help run it for me and talk to my potential clients. It was great fun to stand back and listen to her go on and on about me and my business and why I was the best choice for fitness and why BodSpir® was a revolutionary method of strength training. She was much better at selling me than me! Her faith in me truly helped me to believe in myself.

Another exciting aspect was that I felt I had found a partner for my business. I knew, in the years to come, that I would be doing a lot of traveling, speaking, and running workshops. I needed someone to work with me who I trusted to be as efficient and effective as I would be. That was Elaine. She was detail oriented and understood my business and what was needed. I knew that I would be able to count on her to be by my side, on the road, speaking at gig after gig. And, for her, because of her wealth of knowledge in business and coaching and helping to inspire women, she would be a fabulous speaker as well and the two of us could do a "tag-team" from the stage! What fun we would have. We would both get so excited when we talked about being on the road together. We loved the idea of traveling, speaking, inspiring, and teaching women a way to be their best selves. It was such a gift for each of us that we had found a friend and a business partner to work with as well as play with.

For some of the "playing" part, Elaine would come down to visit me at my home. I, very fortunately, live in a beautiful seaside community, similar to one Elaine lived in for several years. I think coming here made her feel like she was going home. My house is large enough to give her her own bedroom and bath and some privacy. I think she was the only guest I ever had that I did not feel like I had to entertain. She just moved right in and came and went in and around the responsibilities that I had taking care of my mom. For those few years that Elaine would visit, my mom was pretty dependent on me. We shared the house, as she was not able to be on her own. She met Elaine when she was ninety-three and boy, did they hit it off! Especially when there was a Patriots football game on. That was my time to leave as the two of them hooted and hollered and yelled at the TV!

Or, if the weather was nice, we would walk to the beach or have cocktails on the deck. And, we didn't have to do everything together. So, I might take a walk up the beach while she stayed on her beach chair and read her book—or vice-versa. We didn't talk all the time either. Sometimes she would do her thing and I would do mine. Never any pressure to conform or live in acquiescence. And we laughed, boy, did we laugh. Great big belly laughs, whenever we were together. And, SHE laughed, a lot. Actually, all the time. How could someone who brought so much joy to the world not have the chance to do that anymore? How could she be gone? And so suddenly.

There is something to be said about sudden death. There is no plan, there is no anticipation, there are no hypotheticals, there is no waiting. It just happens and all you can do is react the best way you can. There are no rules, no guidelines. The good news is that everyone around you, your support system, will do anything for you. They are in as much shock as you are, but they are not the victim, you are. So, they have to step way outside their comfort zone to be there for you. No one is in charge; you all do the best you can.

Because my son's death was out of the blue, receiving the phone call in the middle of the night, I had experienced one of the worst shocks any parent could face. One day (actually the previous weekend) we were laughing and joking and so happy to spend time together. Then, a hug, a wave goodbye, and blow a kiss with complete naivete that that would be the last time I would ever see him. From the moment of the phone call, for weeks into months on end, I walked around in a bubble. As if life was going on around me, I was functioning in it, but nothing was getting through. The fog I was surviving in was comforting. And, when these shocks occur and other people find out about it, they are even less willing to talk to you than you are to talk to them, which is actually a relief. They don't know what to say, which is great because you don't want to talk anyway. The numbness becomes comfortable and your safety net. Only time helps it to dissipate. Only as time passes does the numbness wane. Some days were easier than others, for no apparent reason. Even now, thirteen years later, there isn't a day that goes by that I don't think about him, but now with warmth and solace rather than emptiness and a void. Time healed that wound. Little did I know that the aftermath of my son's death would happen to me again.

Granted, losing a best friend is certainly not the same as losing a child. And, because we had only known each other for five years, the depth of attachment was not as severe as it could have been had we been friends for decades. But, that fog, that bubble came right back, like an old friend. I knew my limitations and what I was capable of for weeks and months to follow, because I had been through it before, hugely magnified. I was relieved by the familiarity of that state of mind I was able to function in. Losing Elaine, needless to say, was "easier" than losing my son. It's only been two years and the fog has long lifted. I smile at her picture each day and thank her for her love and support as I continue to venture forth with my work. But the experience of losing my son certainly prepared me for what life would be like after a severe loss, like Elaine was to me.

I found out where the memorial service was to be held and arrived about a half hour early. The line was already getting long. I stood quietly, smiling slightly at people who made eye contact. Then a woman entered and got in line behind me. We smiled politely and introduced ourselves. And, as Elaine would have it, this woman was with her when she died. (Elaine wanted to make sure I got the full story from the "horse's mouth.") This friend of hers, in her compassion when she learned who I was, was willing to share all the details of what happened.

Out of respect, I will not share those details here. However, the bottom line, she just stopped breathing. She just died. At sixty-one years old, with no previous medical condition to cause this to happen, she just stopped breathing. As I have tried over the last couple of years to rationalize and justify what happened, I realize I just can't. There is no reasoning that will help to have her death make sense. Certainly, after losing my son, and now Elaine, I know all too well: when it's your time, it's your time. And, on that snowy afternoon in February as she was outdoors, enjoying herself with some friends, it was her time.

After the memorial service for Elaine, I was able to connect with a few of her friends that I met at the service. A couple of them in particular reached out and we Zoomed a few times. Of course, COVID had just gotten started, so the loss of Elaine combined with the loss of freedom made grieving both easier and harder. Easier, because I didn't have to pretend to feel great to anyone as I wasn't really seeing anyone. I lost all my personal training clients, but I did maintain my classes online. Combining all the classes into just two per week, I was able to be upbeat for them.

It was harder because I needed her. I kept reaching out to call her. I kept looking for a text or Facebook post. My mom was driving me crazy, and I needed her to make me laugh. I was stuck—really stuck—with my book and I needed her to talk me through it. (She had actually edited the first round of my book—the entire book of thirteen chapters, she read and edited!) I was low and I needed her to boost me up, to dream big with me. I needed to hear her laugh. The laugh that sometimes drove me crazy cause she laughed so often, I needed to hear that laugh. I missed my friend.

So, I started to talk to her when I took my daily walks. Not long, drawn out conversations, but snippets of them. I would notice a bird or a tree and ask if she saw it, too. Sounds crazy, I know, but it really helped. I was able to imagine that she was there with me, taking that walk. We would go down to the beach and talk about the people there or the surf or the rocks or the pond—anything to connect with her. As time went on, the questions would get a bit more technical and about business. I sensed an answer and would apply it to whatever I was working on. Now, whether it was Elaine answering or me making up the answer in my head, it didn't really matter. As far as I was concerned, there was a conversation taking place with my friend Elaine and, in my mind, I was getting feedback from her. I was connecting with her.

Otherwise, I was pretty alone in my grief. Aside from the two friends of hers I spoke to a few times, there was really no one with whom to share my grief. None of my friends had ever lost a friend, so they couldn't quite identify with what I was going through. When my son was killed, there was no build up to the event—it just happened. One minute he was alive and the next minute he was gone. The same thing happened with Elaine. She was there on Thursday and gone on Saturday. Having lost my son, especially in such an abrupt way, I was all too familiar with loss and grieving and going from everything is fine in one moment to everything is far from fine in the next. I actually think that losing him made it easier to go through losing Elaine. After all, I had lived through the worst grief a person could imagine. She was my friend, not my child. And there are many other friends in my life that I can turn to. But she was my "best" friend at the time:

meaning that she was my "go-to" friend, the first one I would call about anything, the one who I would discuss homelife or business all in the same phone call, the one who expected nothing in return (though I know I was the same for her).

Now, two years later, I really haven't met anyone to take her place. Although it can be lonely sometimes, that has been okay. I do have many women in my life who I call friends and with the COVID restrictions slowly lifting, I am beginning to spread my wings and venture out of my little seaside town and see them in person. And, in those moments of wanting to talk with her, I do anyway. I go back and forth in conversation with her, but I do miss that laugh. Sometimes, when I really focus and close my eyes and envision her in front of me, I can really hear her voice, not just responses in my head, but her voice, her tone, her inflections, and that laugh. It always makes me smile.

As I look back at the time we did have, how could it be that those times were it? That's all we got. Not even five years. How can it be that you will not physically be here for my book launch or the speaking tour? You were supposed to be my right arm and tour with me. We were going to have so much fun going from city to city, book signing to book signing, workshop to workshop. How will I do all that alone? I know you will be there in spirit as I know you are around me now, but the belly laughs and snide comments just aren't the same.

The funny thing is, and continues to be, that I do know she is here with me a lot of the time. I can actually feel her presence. I continue to chat with her, not just on the walks, but throughout the day. Her picture is on my desk, so I look at her on and off all day. I am so blessed that I know in my heart that she is right here with me. I think that the light that shines on my grief is my spiritual belief system.

I believe that those who die don't really go very far. Though we can't see them as a physical presence, does not mean that they are not here. And, for me, I have quite the trifecta: my son, my mom (who passed a year ago at the age of ninety-eight), and my best friend. The three of them are together, supporting me and loving me and believing in me and my gifts that I am sharing with the world. So, if they cannot be here physically, I am still graced by their presence spiritually—every day…until I join them.

CHAPTER 5

Healing Abuse Opens Your Heart
to Unconditional Love

by Joanne Sapers

I remember hearing about women suddenly recalling how somebody had physically and sexually abused them years ago. I felt grateful. I had two parents who loved me very much and two sisters and a brother. We never argued. I loved being happy, and I had a very happy childhood.

I was unaware that happiness was the only emotion I experienced. It's like I had been living in one world. Until, on a particular evening, everything in my life changed forever.

I can't tell you the exact year because so much of my childhood and adulthood is a blur. My daughter and I had moved into my mom and dad's condo. It was around 8:00 p.m. Earlier that day, I had watched Oprah. I was sitting on my bed, and suddenly I felt sick. The kind of sick that makes your head spin. I heard my mind saying, *Oh my God. Is it true?*

My mind was remembering what I saw and heard on Oprah that afternoon. This middle-aged woman shared how she blocked out so much of her childhood and adult memories. Her uncle had sexually abused her. This woman said her parents never did anything to stop the abuse for years.

I ran downstairs and went into my parent's room. Feeling nauseous, I asked my mother about my grandmother's maid named Chutie. Chutie lived with my grandmother for many years. She used to take care of my mother, her two sisters, and her brother when they were children and teenagers. My family lived fifteen minutes from my grandmother, and I was Chutie's favorite child.

The question I asked my mother was, "When did Chutie die?"

My mother said when I was ten years old. My whole body went numb. Intuitively I knew my mother would say that's when Chutie died.

Watching Oprah earlier that day triggered the memories of what had happened to me. I then told my mother what I remembered. I was praying that she would say to me yes, it did happen. My heart was beating fast. I felt like I was going to fall over. What my mother said was "No, it didn't happen."

I felt sick. I now knew my worst fear was confirmed. I went for counseling because I knew I needed support and help.

From birth until Chutie died, Chutie physically and sexually abused me. It would happen when I was alone with her, which was often.

After a few years of counseling, I was ready to stop going. I thought I was all better. I was not. I didn't realize until many decades later that this abuse affected every area of my life.

I was living two lives. When everyone was home, my life felt good. When Chutie took care of me, my life was horrible. She bribed me and threatened me.

It didn't make sense that no one was protecting me. My mother and father were always so loving, quickly saying, "I love you." I thought, *why isn't anyone stopping Chutie? Doesn't God care about me? Aren't I worth loving?*

I felt confused. I learned to block out pain and disassociate myself from my body as a way of coping. I was afraid I would have a nervous breakdown if I ever let myself feel my feelings. For years, I felt unworthy. On the outside, I smiled. I wanted the outside world to tell me I was worth loving. I didn't know how to love myself. I would try to feel better by buying things. I wanted my boyfriends to love me. That way, I would know I was worthy.

The only way I can be willing to write about how Chutie impacted my life is by having a dialog with Spirit. This way, I am being comforted as I write. To report this next section feels very difficult. I find myself surrendering to God for the willingness to go into my memories and feel the hurt, pain, shame, sadness, and especially the fear as I type these words.

As a little girl, I remember feeling small and invisible. I felt like I didn't matter. My little mind was fragile. I believed I was not important because no one stopped Chutie from hurting me. I felt confused and unprotected in this world. The abuse happened at my grandmother's house when I was alone in the house with Chutie. I could feel my throat aching.

As a little girl, I now lovingly called Little Joannee, I remember I would smile so I wouldn't cry. Any happy memories I had ended when someone said the name Chutie.

I felt very unsafe in my body. To exist within these two very diverse life conditions, I developed a way to leave my body anytime I didn't feel safe.

By disassociating myself from being in my body, I decided it was only safe to feel happy. I felt like a victim and saw the world through Victim's thoughts, feelings, and actions. I did everything I could so I wouldn't need to feel.

I lived in my imagination. When I felt nervous, my stomach hurt. I had limited coping skills because I lived with such deep fear of Chutie.

I felt nervous when I didn't understand something. The more I wanted to understand, the more anxious I became. The result was I felt different than my friends. I didn't feel worthy. I compared myself to everyone else.

The bottom line is I didn't feel safe letting myself feel anything that wasn't pleasant. I cried quickly because my ability to feel emotions other than good was practically nonexistent.

I liked being alone, just not alone with my thoughts. I was deathly afraid of what I might think about if I let my feelings come through. I convinced myself that I would probably have a nervous breakdown if I ever felt or heard my thoughts.

Here are some more of the most significant ways and examples of this physical, emotional, and sexual abuse that had affected my life choices. I remember in kindergarten that I compared myself to one little girl. Everyone liked her. I imagined that life was happy all the time for her.

I felt so alone. I felt inner desperation. I found ways to prove to myself how unworthy I was. Then every time I was with Chutie, it confirmed I was not safe, no one was protecting me, and therefore I was unworthy.

I learned many ways to soothe myself physically and emotionally because I believed I was a victim.

I desperately wanted the outside world to validate my worthiness. Instead of learning how to feel my emotions, I found many ways to numb my feelings for decades.

My thinking was extremely black and white. There was no room for me to be gentle or listen to my feelings or thoughts. I was rigid in my beliefs. Here are some examples. I was bulimic with exercise. I would walk eight miles, sixteen miles, and twenty-six miles. I refused to listen to my body even when I was exhausted from walking. I would follow up these long walks with binge eating, stuffing my feelings. I disassociated myself from my body while I was overeating. I didn't know how to feel better.

When it came to dating and love, I didn't know how to make healthy choices. I wanted to be loved so badly. What I wanted from a boy and then from a man: I wanted to feel worthy. I liked this boy telling me he loved me and how special I was because I didn't know how to love myself.

I didn't trust my judgment. I wanted everyone to tell me what would be best for me. I was constantly testing God to see if I was worthy of being alive.

I knew that I needed to see a counselor. I had convinced myself that I would feel great by the end of the first session, and I would never need to have counseling again. It wasn't that way at all. The process was much longer than I could have ever imagined.

I saw this counselor for several years. During the first or second session, she helped me with these memories. She called them flashbacks.

I wasn't willing to feel my emotions or go deep into my past. I couldn't. Trying to remember the abuse was too scary. We did some Eye Movement Desensitization and Reprocessing (EMDR) work which was life-altering in retrospect. I didn't realize that I still had so much healing to do.

The EMDR experience helped me because I saw in my mind a tiny smidgen of what physically happened when Chutie sexually abused me.

I think that was all I wanted to know at that time. I was scared to go deeper into remembering those years of abuse. I got worse when it came to taking care of myself—and loving myself. I felt more frustrated and insecure. The reason was I was still not open to feeling my feelings. I continued numbing myself by self-soothing, buying trinkets, eating sweets or flour products. I wanted to feel loved and loveable more than anything in the world.

Even though this counselor continued to work with me, I never opened up my feelings in a way to allow the healing to take effect. I wasn't ready and couldn't open up. I wasn't willing to learn how to forgive myself.

At seventeen, I hitchhiked to Canada. I also hitchhiked into Boston without money to see if I could safely get home. I sabotaged myself by putting myself in victim situations.

There was the time I was on a bus, heading to classes at Massachusetts College of Art. I wasn't happy. I comforted myself, thinking that I could kill myself when I was thirty years old if my life stayed the same. By the grace of God, I'm still here. Somehow, I survived my unhealthy decisions even though I kept testing the Universe.

One Friday evening, I went out with my friends for Happy Hour. My friend's cousin wanted to come over to my house. He raped me, and I blamed myself for what he did to me.

I had an excellent relationship with my father and expected all men to treat me well. Because of the abuse I endured, I did not choose healthy emotional partners. The men I chose to be with were on their own healing journey. I didn't know how to be a partner or advocate for myself.

I was married four times and found men that I could fix. I saw my first husband as more like a brother than a husband. We were on vacation, sleeping on a beach when I heard a noise. My husband's solution was to give me a rock to throw. I felt unloved. Who is this man that doesn't want to protect me?

When we were engaged, I became pregnant while living in California. I chose to have an abortion. After the abortion, I hemorrhaged and nearly died. He planned to go away that weekend, even though I was recuperating from hemorrhaging. I still chose to marry this man. I did not understand my self-worth. I have forgiven myself for not knowing how to take care of myself.

Our decision to get married was from a place of fun, not from a deep loving commitment. We planned our honeymoon saying to each other if our marriage didn't work out, we would get an amicable divorce. That was our mindset. We had an amicable divorce. Neither one of us knew how to be healthy in a relationship.

If I had healthy boundaries back then, I would have ended this relationship sooner.

Five years later, I started dating a lot and decided I would meet and date maybe four or five guys simultaneously, not be involved with any of them until I knew who I wanted to be with intimately.

Of course, I chose the least healthy man to love. That was my second husband. I still didn't know how to be a good partner. I didn't know how to love myself, and I didn't believe I was lovable and worth loving.

I met my second husband while working at Sikorsky Aircraft in Connecticut. I had a great job with benefits, and he was someone that wanted everything I had. We both wanted to know that we were worth loving.

When we got married, he said, "If you love me, you'll buy me a Dodge Daytona Turbo Z." I didn't know how to drive a stick shift. I still said yes. He told me I should pay for my engagement ring if I love him because he wanted me to have a beautiful ring. That will prove to him that I knew he was successful. He said he would pay me back and never did.

I realized after we were married that I had made a mistake.

I permitted myself to make mistakes and kept sabotaging my relationships by not healing myself and not choosing healthy relationships.

I made what could have been a fatal decision between my second and third marriage. I was engaged to a man for eighteen months. I wanted him to know that he was loveable and life could be good. He became suicidal two weeks before his divorce date. I helped him and told him that we could work everything out through counseling. What happened next was the result of my not knowing how to have healthy boundaries. He came over to my apartment, raped me for four hours, and then suffocated me. I left my body for four minutes and saw the divine light. I said I was ready to go, and then God told me it was not my time to leave the earth plane. "You have service to do." A soft fluffy cloud gently dropped me back into my body. I was gratefully back home.

My third marriage was a disaster. I married my third husband because of how he treated me while we were dating. I ended up getting the flu. After that, I got a lethal autoimmune virus that looked hideous and very painful. I had over eighty boils and blisters all over my body.

I looked like something from Star Trek. It was tough for me to feel okay about myself. I loved that he could love me even though I looked horrible. I knew he wasn't perfect for me. I still said yes and kept dating this man for eight years because he was so loving to me when I was sick.

The gift of this immune virus is that it took me on my holistic healing journey. I wanted to help my body heal. I became a Reiki master, massage therapist, and learned cranial therapy.

I thought being with this man would be excellent for myself and my daughter when I chose to marry him. When I met him, he treated me like gold from day one. Again, I still wanted to be loved and feel good about myself.

It wasn't a good marriage. This man was not kind to his daughter. I needed a restraining order, and I didn't know how to protect myself. I still had more lessons to learn and heal.

I was in the same mode of wanting to fix my fourth husband, and he tried to fix me. I could not speak my truth because I was afraid he would leave me if I shared everything I felt about our relationship. I couldn't share my points of view because I still wanted to be loved more profoundly than I wanted to honor my thoughts, feelings, and soul. This inability to trust kept me feeling like a victim. He was afraid I would be kidnapped or raped if I went out without him. The only way I felt able to stay with him was by immersing myself deeper into my spiritual journey, and my spiritual journey became a number one priority for me.

Finally, decades after the abuse and a lot of healing, I attracted an excellent partner to love. Dave has been the love of my life for over nine years. Dave and I met on the online dating site Plenty of Fish. My fourth husband helped me get on this dating site because he wanted me to be happy and meet someone I could love. My relationship with Dave is all about love, respect, honesty, kindness, caring, and compassion for each other.

I knew there was something extraordinary about Dave when I saw his picture. I had only been on the online dating site, Plenty of Fish, for two weeks. I immediately liked Dave. I could feel from the picture his loving, heartfelt energy, and I knew he was kind and caring. Dave wrote in his dating profile about how he brought his mother, who had Alzheimer's, to live with him in his house. He talked about how he loved his cat, art, flea markets, hiking, and the ocean. Everything that I also loved. I knew I wanted to get to know Dave. He was finishing up a relationship, and we connected by phone two weeks later.

Our very first date felt like it was at Cheers Bar in Boston. Dave picked me up, and we went out for breakfast. Dave knew the owner and everyone that worked at the restaurant. I love so many qualities about Dave. He cares about how everyone is doing, feeling, and their families. Dave is the most loving, caring partner I could ever ask for. Ever since our first date, we have been together. The day I moved in with Dave was the same day his mom transitioned. It was November 1, 2013. I love waking up and going to sleep every day with Dave. We laugh, celebrate each other, honor each other's paths, are compassionate, love hugging and holding each other.

Every day I thank the Universe for bringing us together. Dave is my best friend. He's very different from me regarding my deep level of spirituality. I study philosophy, seek to know and learn quantum physics, energy and understand our universe from an intensely spiritual place. Yet Dave is my soulmate. He is the perfect partner for me. We are there for each other, and I love and adore him. Dave knows that I am a perpetual learner. When I was studying to become a licensed spiritual practitioner, he was with me and understood when I put my practitioner license on hold. Whatever is important to Dave, I'm right here to offer support, love, guidance and see his dreams manifest, as he is for me.

I'm very grateful Dad and Dave had time to get to know each other. I know Dad is thrilled that I finally see myself with love, believe in myself, and choose a loving partner that is just right for me. When I told Dad about Dave, Dad's heart lit up! I am so grateful to be with Dave, the love of my life.

My Healing and Where I Am Today

It's been a long road, and I understand and appreciate every experience I've had, which has taken me to where I am today. Some of these most challenging experiences are the ones that helped wake me up. For example, when the man I was engaged to tried to kill me, I woke up enough to realize that I needed to do a lot of inner work. That may seem obvious to you, yet it was an "aha" moment for me.

I was blessed to grow up with a wonderful mother and father that did everything for their four children. I have always felt loved by Mom and Dad and my loving siblings. By forgiving and opening my heart to unconditional loving, I had the gift to stay with my mother and nurse her back to health in August 2021 when she fell backward and hit her head. She was ninety-five years young at the time. I feel so blessed that we had that sacred mother/daughter time together. There was so much healing that went on during that month.

Dad passed in 2020. I had an excellent relationship with my father. I believe that all men in my life wanted the best for me. Dad and I loved each other unconditionally.

Growing up loved by Mom and Dad, the forgiveness of others has come easily to me. I am grateful to have this gift. It has allowed me to forgive Chutie and my parents. The most difficult person for me to forgive has been myself.

Somehow by the grace of God, even though I was told it would be very difficult for me to get pregnant, I received a miracle, my daughter, Alisa. Alisa, thank you for being my "why" when I didn't know what I didn't know. Even though you are my daughter, you continue to be one of my biggest teachers. I love you with all my heart! I'm so proud of the loving and kind person you are. I thank God for giving me the most beautiful heartfelt soul daughter I could ever imagine! I love you, your wonderful husband, Kevin, and our two grandchildren, Benji and Lilly!

I love sharing every day with Dave, my best friend and the love of my life, and now my husband! We just got married in Hawaii on April 10, 2022.

Through Dave, I am blessed with our third grandson, Aiden, and Dave's daughter. I truly have the most loving family, friends, colleagues, clients, and life!

I thank God every day that I am so willing and desire to forgive myself and others, without exception.

The tools that have helped me heal are listed below.
- I called the rape crisis line many times in the middle of the night.
- I went for counseling.
- My counselor did a therapy called Eye Movement Desensitization and Reprocessing (EMDR) with me. I remember I felt the beginning of a new sense of peace.
- I went to the twelve-step codependency group for a while.
- I went to the twelve-steps Overeaters Anonymous for thirteen years to help me with my emotional eating disorder.

- I became a Reiki master to help myself heal and help others.
- I became a licensed massage therapist to help myself connect to my own body and help others.
- I learned cranial therapy to help myself and others.
- I took over thirty self-development classes and programs.
- I read and listen to self-love and self-development books.

I joined the Center for Spiritual Living and became a licensed spiritual practitioner for four years. These four years and the years of studying deepened my relationship with God. I am a lifetime spiritual practitioner now. My relationship with God is the most important relationship I have. I meditate daily, read spiritual literature, and believe what we think we create.

I feel infinitely blessed to see the good in myself and all. When I left my body for four minutes, I received a gift that filled me with joy. I can hear what someone's heart wants them to know for their highest and best. As a spiritual love relationship coach and visionary, I am beyond grateful to help women love themselves unconditionally one day at a time.

Anyone who knows me knows that I think love is the most beautiful word in our language. I'm here to see anyone and everyone as love. I know we are all on our unique journey.

I love being a love relationship coach and helping women learn how to forgive themselves and others. Celebrate who they are from the inside out and love themselves in ways they never thought were possible.

CHAPTER 6

The Journey into the Unknown

In loving memory of Ronald F. DeSisto
September 12, 1953 to January 20, 2008

by Carleen DeSisto

July 5, 2007 is a day I will never forget. It was the day that I brought my husband, Ron, to an outpatient facility wherein a surgeon would perform a procedure that would enable him to obtain access to a mass located near Ron's lung. The plan was to make an incision in his neck which would allow the doctor to get under his breastbone and locate the mass. Prior to this procedure, two other attempts had taken place to locate the mass in May and June in which the doctors were not successful. The first procedure was attempted through his nose and the second procedure was attempted through his throat. Two months had gone by since the results of a chest scan taken in May indicated that there was a mass, and we still didn't know whether the mass was cancerous.

The third attempted procedure was successful. The surgeon was able to locate the mass near his lung and remove cell samples that could be biopsied. When the surgery was completed, the surgeon came out to speak with me and tell me what he found. The results were not what I wanted to hear. In addition to the mass, which I will now call a tumor, he found some abnormal-looking cells. His preliminary diagnosis was that, in his opinion, the tumor appeared to be cancerous and most likely malignant. He also told me that the tumor was inoperable because of where it was located. He believed that the biopsy results would confirm his diagnosis. After speaking with the surgeon, I turned to my mom, who surprised me earlier by coming to the outpatient facility so that I wouldn't be alone when I got the news. She took one look at me and gave me a big hug and just held me while I broke down in her arms. I was in a state of shock and knew in my gut that my life would never be the same from this point on. This was the beginning of my journey into the unknown. My whole life seemed to flash before me. Prior to the procedure my gut told me that it wasn't going to be good news, but I hoped for the best. Seeing his body deteriorate day in and day out was breaking my heart. He had lost so much weight because of his inability to eat and drink. I did my best not to show him how stressed I was feeling. The thought of losing my best friend kept me up at night.

It seemed like the results were taking forever. It was all I could think about. Approximately ten days later the doctor's office called to make an appointment. The doctor would tell us the results when we met with him. After receiving the call, I knew in my heart that the news was going to be that it was cancer. My nightmare was coming true. I tried to be positive, but it was so hard. I was overwhelmed with emotions. How bad was it? Was it a matter of months or a year? Would he have to be hospitalized for his treatments? I tried to push the thoughts out of my mind. The appointment couldn't come fast enough. I kept myself distracted with work and going to the gym. It was difficult focusing while I was in work. I found myself staring at the computer screen at times in a daze. One of my coworkers lost her husband to cancer so it helped being able to talk to her and tell her how terrifying it was not knowing whether he would survive the disease.

The day of reckoning arrived. The doctor came into the room and revealed the results of the biopsy. The tumor was cancerous, and it was inoperable due to its location. He recommended seeing an oncologist as soon as possible as the cancer was already in stage four. I felt like fainting. There was no more denying the inevitable. The type of cancer was small cell adenoma carcinoma, which was not aggressive but would spread over time. Since he was in stage four, the chance that it spread to other areas of his body was highly likely. Again, not what I wanted to hear. I was in shock and just going through the motions while trying to be supportive, but all I really wanted to do was scream and shout, "Why is this happening to me?" He was a smoker and had been for a long time. Deep down I always felt that his smoking would come to haunt me one day. I prayed that it wouldn't come to be, and here we were in this place in time. I needed the comfort and support of my family and close friends to get through this. I knew that they would be there for me. Even though I wasn't the one diagnosed with cancer, I still needed help to deal with my emotions. If he did succumb to the cancer, where would that leave me? There were so many thoughts running through my mind.

We met with the oncologist, and he confirmed that this type of cancer was a spreader. The first thing that needed to be done was to run additional tests to determine if the cancer was in other parts of his body. Once the results were in, he would be able to establish the treatment protocol. I can't remember how long it was before the results of the tests were in, but it seemed like forever. All I could think about was a worst-case scenario. I continued to work full time. I just couldn't sit home and wait. Did I feel guilty leaving him alone while I went to work? You bet I did; however, I needed to do it for my emotional well-being.

The test results showed that the cancer had indeed spread to his abdomen, left forearm, and left upper leg, and had already metastasized to his bones; hence the stage four diagnosis. That news was heart wrenching. I think my first question to the doctor was, "If this is a slow-moving cancer, how long do you think he has had it?" The doctor's guess was approximately two years. Then I asked, "What are his chances of survival?" The doctor's response was that it depended upon how his body reacted to the chemo regiment, but if he had to make an educated guess, probably 44 percent of a chance. That remark hit me like a ton of bricks! I was still in shock and probably didn't comprehend everything that he said.

I was able to take a couple of hours out of work and go with him to all his doctor's appointments. Initially I sat with him while he was getting his chemo treatments. Never in a million years did I picture myself in this position. I wanted to be there to comfort him, but it got to be too much for me. The sight of the chemo bag dripping into the tube and going into his body was too emotional for me. Instead of sitting next to him, I would drop him off and come back when the treatment was finished. Then I would get into my car and go off to work. Going back and forth was taking a toll on me, but I continued to do it as long as it didn't interfere with my job. Thankfully I had some flexibility and an understanding boss.

It was very stressful for me to be working full time and leave him every day, but I knew I needed the distraction. I couldn't imagine what he was going through and wanted to be as supportive as I could be, but mentally it was taking a lot out of me, and I felt guilty. I didn't want him to see that side of me, so I didn't share how I was feeling with him. I was able to share my feelings with one of my coworkers who lost her husband to cancer and to a couple of close friends and family. I wanted to be strong for him and give him hope. Even though I felt in my heart that our time was limited, I was in denial and didn't want to believe it. I also continued my regiment of going to the gym at least three times a week which helped work out some of the stress and to get some hugs and support from my gym friends. A few of us would go to Honey Dew Donuts on Saturdays after class and sit and chat for about an hour.

During the fall season he continued to lose weight. He was feeling more nauseous and fatigued from the treatments. I would continually ask the doctor during his appointments if the chemo was working. I wasn't feeling positive about the situation due to his lack of progress and wanted to know if it was because the cancer was spreading. I was always the one asking the questions of the doctor. Ron seemed to just take it in stride, and he continued to believe that he would beat the cancer. In response to my questions about the lack of progress, the doctor suggested he take a month off from the chemo and then he would reevaluate. That was the best month we had in a long time. I was hopeful that his body just needed a break and that his situation would improve. In hindsight I should have taken some time off and planned a short get away. But we can't go back in time.

In December he woke up one morning in excruciating pain. His neck was very stiff, and it was hard to get out of bed. The first thing I thought of was, *the cancer is spreading again.* My stress levels were increasing, and my hope was diminishing that he would come through this episode positively. My gut feeling proved to be true. The results of the scan showed that the cancer had spread to the top of his back near the neck area. Once again, he would have to endure radiation treatments once a day for several weeks.

The holidays were fast approaching, and I kept thinking that this could be the last Christmas that we share together. How could that be happening to me? Again, I didn't share my feelings with him. I didn't want to give up hope, but as the days passed, he was was becoming weaker and more fatigued, and was in a lot of pain from the radiation burning his skin. The doctor put him on morphine pills to help minimize the pain. I started to work from home so that I could be there for him. I didn't want to give up because he still had such a positive attitude and looked at this as just a setback. He truly believed that he would be around for a couple of more years. I wanted to believe that too, but I could see how much his body was deteriorating and there wasn't anything I could do about it. His weight loss started in March of 2007. Now nine months later, he'd lost around seventy pounds.

As it got closer to Christmas, I could hardly get him to eat or drink. It hurt too much. I was getting more and more depressed, but I didn't want to show it. One of our traditions was to buy presents for each other and open them on Christmas morning. He told me that he wouldn't be able to go shopping for me this year and he felt bad about it. I told him not to worry and that I was just happy to spend time with him. That's when it really hit me. This could very well be our last Christmas together. I didn't want him to feel bad, so I spoke to my mom about it. I told her that I was thinking of buying some presents for myself and asked her if she would wrap them for me. She thought that was a great idea. A few days before Christmas I came home with some presents and told him that my mom did some shopping for him. It made him so happy, and it made me smile! I was able to make Christmas special and continue our tradition.

January came and he continued with the chemo treatments. It was time to go for his follow up appointment with his doctor. As usual the doctor took blood, weighed him, and then we chatted. I remember being very concerned that day because he was still losing weight and he ate very little. I asked the doctor point blank whether he thought we should be continuing with the chemo treatments. He gave me another vague response and I insisted that he be more specific. I asked him if it were his spouse in this situation, what would he do? I was desperate and scared. I needed answers. Without committing one way or another he said that it was likely that the cancer was continuing to spread. He could schedule some tests that would indicate if that was in fact happening. I discussed it with Ron, and we agreed to go that route. If the tests determined that the cancer was spreading, then we had a tough decision to make. Ron was still in denial. This would be a conversation for later.

The tests were scheduled for Monday, January 21, 2008. I was not looking forward to the conversation with his doctor once the results were in. My heart was telling me that the tests would conclude that the chemo treatments were not helping, and that the cancer was still spreading. If that happened, he would be taken off of chemo and placed on hospice until he passed which could be days or a couple of months. My world was officially turning upside down and sideways! I couldn't imagine being a widow at the age of fifty-one.

I continued to work from home, feeling more and more guilty about it, and as a result, my work suffered. I just couldn't focus. What was I going to do without him in my life? I didn't want to think about it and tried to push it out of my mind.

It was a cold night on January 19, 2008, and Ron wanted to light a fire in the fireplace. It had been quite a while since he had the energy or desire to build and tend a fire. I asked him if he felt like eating. To my surprise he wanted me to cook him supper. I was delighted and excited! I placed his dinner on a TV tray near the fireplace. He ate almost everything on his plate! I felt a glimmer of hope! If he could continue to eat, maybe he would regain his strength and I would have more time to spend with him. But was this realistic? Probably not.

I felt the need to cuddle with him. I couldn't remember the last time we sat together and cuddled while watching television by the fireplace. The warmth of the fire was so comforting. I didn't want to think about the fact that in two days he would be undergoing tests which would likely confirm that that the cancer was still spreading. We talked a bit about the doctor's prognosis, and he was still so positive that he would have more time, while my gut continued to tell me that time was short. I told him that I didn't want him to worry about me if the time came and that I would be okay. I wasn't ready to let him go, but I felt he needed to hear it. Seeing him get worse was eating me alive. I was so proud of his determination to beat this awful disease, and I wanted to be there for him. That was one of the most difficult times that I had faced so far—telling him that it was okay to give in. My heart was aching, and I wanted to break down, but I kept on a happy face.

The following day, January 20, 2018, I went to the gym to destress. When I came home, he asked me to cook him pancakes! I was thrilled that he wanted to try and eat something solid. I again had the thought that if he was getting his appetite back, maybe I really would have more time with him. I gave him a big bear hug and kiss and he smiled at me, and I smiled back. I took joy in the moment.

After breakfast was finished, I went downstairs to shower. After I finished my shower, I went over to check on him. He was sitting in the recliner next to the fireplace and he didn't look well. I asked him how he was feeling. He told me that he was feeling nauseous, and that he had a burning sensation in his chest. I gave him a basin just in case he needed to vomit and then I went upstairs to get dressed. While I was upstairs, I had an uneasy feeling that he wasn't okay. I quickly finished getting dressed and didn't take the time to dry my hair.

I went downstairs and was shocked to find him slumped to one side in the recliner. It couldn't have been more than ten minutes or so since I went upstairs. I immediately panicked and didn't know what to do. I paced back and forth a couple of times. I took another look at him and there wasn't any movement. I shook him and there was no reaction. I wasn't sure if he was breathing. I tapped him in the face and raised his arms. There was still no reaction. I frantically ran to the phone and called 911. When I hung up, I immediately called my brother to tell him what had happened. I didn't want to be alone.

I don't know how long it took for the EMTs to get to my house, but it seemed like an hour. When they finally arrived, I told them he was downstairs. They asked me a bunch of questions and told me to stay upstairs while they worked on him. My brother came shortly thereafter and went downstairs to talk to the EMTs. Then my sister-in-law came in and went downstairs. I have no recollection as to how long they worked on him. While this was happening, I remember being upstairs by myself, sitting on the floor, curled up in a fetal position and screaming hysterically. I was beside myself with emotion. I couldn't believe this was happening. I was not ready for this moment.

Our golden retriever, Jasmine, was downstairs while this was going on. My guess is that she was watching their every move and that she knew something was wrong. I heard someone say "Get the dog out of the room." Shortly after that, they came upstairs and told me that he was alive and that they were taking him to the hospital. I was in a fog and scared to death. My sister-in-law took me to her car, and we followed the ambulance to the emergency entrance of the hospital.

As we were approaching the entrance, I saw the EMTs take him out of the ambulance on a stretcher. He was hooked up to a machine. I remember seeing his chest go up and down so unnaturally. Never in my life had I ever experienced anything like this. It was traumatic to say the least. I was escorted into the waiting area which was outside of the room that he was in.

So many thoughts were going through my mind. Could they keep his heart beating? If they did, would he be conscious or in a coma? Is he suffering and in pain? I prayed for help. I don't know how long it was before the doctor came out and asked me if I wanted them to continue to try to revive him since he had been without oxygen for quite a while. There I was having to make a life-or-death decision in a matter of minutes. So many thoughts rushed through my head. My first reaction was *yes, continue to work on him.* But then I thought of how much he had suffered already and there was no guarantee that if they revived him, he would be able to survive without the help of a machine and whether he would wake up at all and remain in a coma. It was an extremely difficult decision to make.

After processing all the information that they gave me as to what the result could be if they continued and were successful in reviving him, I came to the decision that I had to let him go and end his suffering and pain. I couldn't live with myself if I said yes, and he ended up being hooked up to a machine for the remainder of his life. It hurt like hell, but it was the right thing to do. He suffered enough and it was time for him to be at peace.

They let me go into the room to say goodbye to him. My brother and sister-in-law came in the room with me. I asked for a priest to come in and say some prayers. I touched his face and his body and silently said goodbye. I don't remember how long I stayed in the room before we left. I will never forget how pale and lifeless he looked. That memory will stay etched in my mind forever.

The next thing I needed to do was to go to my parents' house and tell them that he had passed. I was silent on the way there. When we entered the house, my mom and dad immediately knew that something had happened. I broke down in their arms. Both of my parents broke down as well. It was an extremely emotional time for all of us. I gave them the details as best I could and stayed there with my brother and sister-in-law for quite a while.

The Patriots game was on the television at my parents' house. One of my sisters and her family attended the game. I didn't want to break the news to them until they came home. I don't remember who texted them to ask when they would be home. I waited at my parents' house until they were back.

The minute they saw me enter their home with my brother, they knew something bad had happened to Ron. I think my sister said something like "No, don't tell me he's gone" and I shook my head. She instantly came to me with tears in her eyes and hugged me. My sister, her husband, and my niece and nephew were all there. It became a crying fest! Her kids were like my own. They both loved Uncle Ron very much! We had spent a lot of time together on family trips, Little League, soccer, etc.

It was a very emotional day for me relaying the sad news in person and over the telephone. After contacting relatives, close friends, and Ron's boss, it was time to call the funeral home and make an appointment for the next day to go over the arrangements. I wasn't looking forward to making that call. When that task was finished, I sat down, took a deep breath, and curled up on the sofa with the television on to distract me. I just wanted to be alone with Jasmine, my golden retriever, and try to comprehend what I had been through that day.

Words cannot fully express the emotions I was feeling. I thought about the fact that tomorrow, January 21, Ron was scheduled for tests to determine the status of the cancer. The next step would have been making the decision to discontinue the chemo treatments and put him on hospice and wait for him to die. I didn't have to make that decision. A massive heart attack took his life the day prior. I was still in shock.

Selfishly I wanted more time with him, but I didn't get my wish. My entire world was officially turned upside down and sideways. I had to face realty even though I didn't want to do it. I just lost my soulmate, and I knew that my life was going to change dramatically. What was I going to do? I guess I could take one day at a time and put one foot in front of the other and go on from there; however long that would take me. It wasn't the time to make impulse decisions. Thankfully I had the support of family and close friends to help me through the process.

I was exhausted both mentally and physically. The minute I put my head on the pillow that night, my mind was racing with hundreds of thoughts. I couldn't fall asleep no matter what I did. I stayed in bed and waited for the morning to arrive. It was early in the morning when I got up and made myself some tea. Today was the day I would meet with the funeral director. This was not something I wanted to do alone. My parents offered to come with me for moral support. I can still picture myself walking around the room with my parents and Jamie, the funeral director, where the caskets were displayed. What was I going to choose? There were so many different kinds, from plain and simple to very elaborate with carvings. This wasn't my first time picking out a casket, but I never thought I would be doing this now for my husband. He was only fifty-four years old! We had never discussed funeral arrangements and I was at a loss and overwhelmed in having to make all these decisions. I finally chose one that I thought suited him. I remember it had tree carvings on it.

After the choice was made, Jamie led us back to his office to fill out all the necessary paperwork and finalize the day and times for the wake and funeral and write his obituary. That was something that I had never done for anyone! He had a template that I could follow to get me started. It took me quite a while to accomplish this task. Talk about emotional! Picking out a casket was a piece of cake compared to writing an obituary about your husband.

After all the funeral arrangements had been made, we still had to pick out some flowers and finalize the arrangements with my church. Thank God for Mom! She helped me with the flowers and took care of all the music selections for church. With the help of family all the arrangements were completed, and I could go back home.

Waiting until the day of the wake was not easy and was very stressful. I don't remember what I did to pass the time, but what I do remember is that family members kept in touch with me, helped me pick out pictures and put them on boards to be displayed at the wake, and came to my house to just be with me.

The day of the wake arrived. I didn't want to dress in all black. Instead, I chose a simple two-piece brown suit. We arrived at the funeral home early to set up the pictures. I went in the viewing room and knelt by his casket and just looked at him. Then I touched his face and hands and stood next to him for a while. I can still picture how he looked. That memory will never go away. I thought to myself that he was at peace and no longer suffering.

My body felt numb while I was in the receiving line waiting for people to come. I tried to think of good memories to get me through the day. All my immediate family was there to support me throughout the day and evening. It was a day of hugs and tears and very emotional. I anticipated that tomorrow would be a very difficult day and I wasn't looking forward to saying goodbye. The thought of no longer being able to physically see or hold him in my arms was very traumatic. That would be something I would have to learn how to live with for the rest of my life. I don't remember if we went out to eat after the wake or had take-out or who brought me home that night or how long they stayed to keep me company. I do know that I wanted to be alone in my own house with my golden retriever at my side. Did I watch television? Did I get any sleep that night? I don't remember.

I do remember the limousine picking me up the next day and bringing me to the funeral home. Again, I don't remember if it was just me in the limo or if there were family members with me. I entered the room where Ron was being waked and went to be by his side. I stayed there for a while and just looked at him until it was time to stand in line and wait for visitors to come to me. My body still felt numb while I was going through the motions. The priest came and said some prayers. Then it was time to leave the funeral home and head to the church for the funeral. Before it was time for me to go, I went to his casket and knelt in front of it for a bit. This would be the last time I saw his face and be able to physically touch him. This brought tears to my eyes. His body was so cold. I knew it was just his physical body there and that his spirit would be alive in my heart, but it was still hard to leave the room.

I entered the church and walked down the aisle to the front pew. My brother was on the left side of me and one of my sisters was on my right side. I don't remember the music that was playing but it was nice. I remember feeling very sad and that I had tears in my eyes throughout the entire service. The one song that I do remember was "On Eagle's Wings." It had a profound affect on me.

When the mass was over and it was time to leave the church, I broke down as I watched the ushers start to wheel the casket down the aisle. I grabbed my brother's and sister's arms for support. I couldn't stop crying and my body was shaking. It was such a traumatic experience. That's the last thing I remember until we got to the cemetery. I don't remember exiting the church, getting into the limo, or the drive there. My next memory is being near the casket with my family and hearing the priest recite some prayers. What happened when he was finished, I have no clue. I don't remember if we had a reception or when I went home. My guess is that we did have a reception, but I have no memory of what happened the rest of the day. Maybe someday I will, but if I don't, that's okay too. I believe some memories are just so painful to relive that our mind blocks them out to help us heal.

I stayed out of work for two weeks after the funeral. In hindsight I probably should have stayed out longer. I couldn't sleep. I was tired and felt drowsy, but the minute I put my head on the pillow I was wide awake. Because I was feeling sleep deprived, I called my doctor and he prescribed something to help me sleep. After a few days it did start to take affect and I was able to get at about four hours of sound sleep. That still wasn't enough, but it helped.

Going back to work kept me busy and distracted during the day, but it was so hard to focus while I was there. One of the things that helped was talking to a co-worker that lost her husband to cancer several years before me. I could express to her how I was really feeling, and she would give me a hug. She understood a lot of what I was going through and told me to not feel guilty. Just talking to her and hearing her stories was helpful. I also spoke to a few other women who had spouses that died at a young age from cancer. Those conversations helped me to get through the day. When I came home from work, however, I felt lonely and lost. Thank God I had my golden retriever, Jasmine, to greet me and cuddle with.

After dinner I would go downstairs and put the television on. Many times, a certain scene would come on and I would tear up. When that happened, I would text or email my friend in Florida and tell her how I was feeling. It seemed that whenever I saw couples together whether it was on television, in church, or at an event, I became sad and emotional. It reminded me that I was no longer part of a couple and that I wouldn't be growing old with my best friend by my side. Sometimes I would think of vacations that we wouldn't be taking together. It made me feel sad.

I decided to go back to church on a weekly basis and it seemed to give me some comfort by attending. It still made me tear up when I went, especially when the organist played the song "On Eagle's Wings" because the song reminded me of the day of the funeral. That was one of the songs that was played that day. I call these type of occurrences "triggers" and sometimes they would hit me hard.

People were always suggesting that I join a support group to help deal with my grief. That was something that just didn't appeal to me. I had a support group made up of my family and a few close friends. Whenever I felt down or sad, I could reach out to any one of them at any time. That worked for me. I tried to read books on grief, but I didn't find them helpful either. They were too scientific and not personal enough. I continued with my exercise routine which did help to relieve some of my stress. It was a haven where I didn't have to talk to anyone if I didn't want to do so. It was just me and the music and the exercise routine. I didn't have to think about anything else but the steps while I was there. However, if I wanted to reach out, I could. My best friend went to the same gym, and she was always there to give me a hug.

One thing I realized is that people wanted to reach out but didn't know how to or what to say. They didn't want to upset me by saying the wrong thing, so they didn't say anything and even avoided me. Gradually the phone stopped ringing and the small talk decreased. About a month after the funeral, it was like radio silence except for my support group. There were times at work when individuals would see me and walk the other way so they didn't have to ask me how I was doing. Sometimes all I wanted to hear was "Hi, I was thinking about you today." A text message or an email occasionally would have been nice or a card. I did receive a boat load of sympathy cards, and that helped and made me smile, especially when someone took the time to write a personal note. Much later I learned that I needed to be the one to break the radio silence and approach them and tell them it was okay to ask me how I was doing. If I didn't want to talk about something, I would let them know that it was still too raw. I did find out who my true friends were because they frequently kept in touch. There were, however, many times when all I wanted was to be alone with my thoughts. After all my life was changed dramatically, and it was up to me to learn how to cope with it or be forever sad.

I discovered that there were so many things that need to be taken care of shortly after a spouse dies such as removing his name from the bills and putting my name on them. Some companies just needed it in writing while others needed a copy of his death certificate. I had to review his budget plan and figure out a new one now that there would be just one salary and less money coming in to pay bills. Luckily, I was familiar with budgeting and knew where all his papers were so that I could take over. Another task that was necessary and cumbersome was to settle his estate. I hired a lawyer to help me deal with the legal issues. One of the more complex issues that I had to deal with was removing his name from the timeshare that we owned in Florida. Talk about paperwork! It was stressful and overwhelming all at the same time!

Asking for help was not easy for me. I was used to doing things on my own and didn't want to be a pest. What I learned was that asking for help opened the communication channel. When I approached some-one with my ask, they were so happy that I contacted them. My husband always took care of the upkeep of our yard and inground pool. The first time that I went to the pool company after he passed was traumatic even though it had been almost six months since he passed. I explained that I didn't know the first thing about maintaining my pool as my husband always took care of it and he had passed. They were so supportive and helped me get through my first summer. My neighbor helped me figure out which direction the valves on the filter needed to be so that I could use the manual vacuum. I took a picture of the valves to assist me the next time I had to use the vacuum. She was so happy that she could help me.

Another example was learning how to operate and maintain a riding tractor lawn mower. I had no clue as to what to do. I told my good friend about my dilemma, and she volunteered to come over to my house and show me how to not only operate the tractor, but she changed the oil, filter, and spark plug.

Another task that I was not looking forward to doing was taking the trash and the recyclables to the transfer station and using the truck. I was afraid that I would hit something while backing the truck out of the garage. I told my brother about it, and he volunteered to help me with this task until I was comfortable doing it myself. What a relief! Who knew that I would have to master these tasks as well as many others, but I took the reins and plowed through and learned that it was okay to ask for help.

One of the things that bothered me was that people assumed that I would be selling my house because they thought it would be too much for me. I loved my house and my neighborhood. Why would I want to move? I would tell them that I wouldn't be making any impulsive decisions and that I liked my house and if I could afford staying there, why wouldn't I? I had a good paying job with great benefits and both of us had been contributing to 401K plans for a very long time. We were on the fifteen-year plan as to the mortgage on the house and there was only two years left in payments. They didn't even know my financial situation, and yet they were assuming that I couldn't handle it by myself. I was determined to prove them wrong. I was an educated, independent, and strong woman, and I was okay living by myself with my trusted golden retriever. I'm sure that they didn't intend on annoying me, but their statements did just that. I decided to take one day at a time and continue with my routine.

I did a lot of yard work in the spring on the weekends to stay busy and occupy my time. However, I didn't take enough breaks and would be out there for three to four hours at a time. That wasn't one of my best decisions. As a result, I ended up having sciatica issues which alerted me to the fact that I needed to adjust my routine and slow down. I was obsessed with getting all the yard work done by myself. My body was in physical pain, and I couldn't continue down that path. It forced me slow down and get help for some of the tasks. I loved to garden, so I concentrated on that and was able to get a relative to help with the yard work. Not only did my mind need to heal but my body did as well. Lesson learned.

As time went on, work was getting more and more stressful. The financial institution that I worked at was planning on some major layoffs due to what was happening in the country. The stock market was crashing, homes were being foreclosed, the economy was not strong. I survived the first round of layoffs that occurred in 2008; however, there were a lot of changes being made in the financial industry. Mergers were happening, companies were downsizing, and that resulted in me having several manager changes during 2008 and 2009.

Eventually the decision was made to consolidate managers in my business line, and they eliminated my position. My staff would now be reporting to a manager located in Boston. Fortunately, my boss had an open slot for a project manager and offered me the position. The bad news was that I would no longer be reporting to my current manager, who I enjoyed working with because she was very supportive of me. I ended up reporting to a colleague of mine and dropping a level in the hierarchy. I had been a senior vice president, and she was a vice president. As a result, my officer title was reduced to a vice president. I was extremely upset, but I didn't have a choice. I needed my job.

It took quite awhile to get used to my new position and working for my colleague. That change put additional stress on my already stressful life. I struggled through and did the best that I could. However, more changes were to come. Another merger happened and their managers took over our business line. I was put in a pool of employees who were waiting to be chosen for another position. I ended up reporting to a person who was in New Jersey and a lot younger than me. This was her first manager role.

The next few months didn't go well. I was given menial tasks to complete, and it was a blow to my ego. I was used to being the "go-to person" and now I worked on spreadsheets. I was not happy in this position, and I dreaded going to work every day. Layoffs continued to occur. I no longer had the support of a manager that knew what my skill sets were. To top things off, in April of 2009, I came down with shingles! Just what I needed.

It was so painful, and I was all alone. Mom offered to come over to help me get through it.

I don't remember a lot of the details as to how I felt from day to day. It felt like I was just going through the motions and dealing with the grief as best as I could. I spent a lot of time at home during the summer months. I sat by the pool and daydreamed while my golden retriever enjoyed swimming in the pool. I tried to think of happy memories, but it was difficult. There was still so much to process! I continued taking medication to sleep. I kept a lot inside and didn't share how I was feeling. I wanted to move forward but that was easier said than done. Work was still not going well, and I feared that I would lose my job. My heart just wasn't into it anymore.

It was a struggle to get up every morning. I spent a lot of time teary-eyed. The toughest times, however, were the weekends. I was alone and my thoughts would drift. Sometimes I felt guilty that I didn't spend more time with him while he was sick. I questioned whether he would have survived longer if I insisted he consult with doctors in Boston instead of seeing a local oncologist. Why didn't I tell him the reasons for me continuing to work full time? The list went on and on and was making me more and more depressed. I kept thinking about things I wouldn't be able to do any more instead of thinking about what I could do. I usually traded my car in every four to five years. In September I decided that I could afford to keep on with my tradition and bought a new car. I did something that made me feel good.

Whenever I felt lonely or sad, I allowed myself to express my feelings. I didn't hold back. Sometimes when I came home from a stressful day at work, I just wanted to be alone with my feelings and cuddle with my golden retriever. Other times I would immerse myself into cooking. If I felt like crying, I did just that. If I wanted to talk to someone, I could reach out to one of my family members or close friends. They were my support group. Some people encouraged me to go to a formal support group, but I never did. That type of support was not what I wanted or needed.

The holidays were fast approaching, and I was not looking forward to them. This would be the second Christmas without him. I got through last year by just going through the motions. I wasn't in the celebrating mood. Two weeks before Christmas I received a phone call from my boss, telling me that my position was eliminated and that I was being let go and that I could leave that day. I had been working there for twenty-seven years and that's how my career was ending. I was so distraught and upset that this was how they chose to let me go. I was just a number to them. I was given a one-year severance package which meant I would get my salary and the cost of my medical coverage would not increase. At least I had a year to decide what I wanted to do next. As usual I hosted Christmas Eve. It was very hard, but I pushed through. Having my family with me meant a lot to me.

During the following year, I concentrated on taking care of myself. I adopted a new perspective on life wherein I wouldn't let little obstacles bother me anymore. I wasn't going to worry about what my future would look like. Instead of going to the gym two to three times a week, I started working out four to five times per week. It helped not only physically but mentally as well.

I decided to take a vacation by myself and book a week at my timeshare in Florida. I knew it wouldn't be easy, but I was determined to take on this new adventure. I had to prove to myself that I could do things without him and continue to live my life. Even though I had flown by myself several times over the years for work, it was a stressful experience. I kept telling myself that this would be good for me, and that I needed the down time to help me through the grieving process. This was going to be a trip of firsts for me, i.e., driving a rental car an hour and a half and navigating the trip to the resort at night; checking in alone and being asked if anyone would be joining me; and deciding whether to order in or go out to a restaurant and ask for a table for one.

My stay at the resort did help me with the grieving process. I was able to reenergize and think about what I had been through. I took long walks along the beach and listened to the sound of the ocean. I didn't want to be sad all the time and think about all the things that I would no longer experience as a couple. He was gone, but I was still here. He would want me to move on. I tried to think of the happy memories and compartmentalize the sad memories. It was easier said than done, but it did help. I kept myself busy and concentrated on things that I could accomplish that made me happy and not sad. For a long time, it was hard to talk about him without shedding tears.

Visiting my parents after my exercise class on Saturday's became one of my routines. I looked forward to it each week. It was a safe place for me. Sometimes I would reminisce with them about some of the fun things Ron and I did together like what we did on one of our vacations. Other times I would just watch television with my dad or do some gardening with my mom. One spring I decided to plant a vegetable garden for my dad. Gardening was very cathartic for me. It gave me a purpose and satisfaction and became one of my happy places. My dad was thrilled about having a garden and that gave me joy too.

As time went on, I learned how to ease into conversations and be more open and talk about him with less tears. Texts, emails, and phone calls to and from my close friends and family were my saving graces. Many times, when I was feeling sad, I would send an email of what was going through my mind to my good friend in Florida. She would either call me or email a response that was supportive and caring. She would also check in with me on a continual basis and just say something like "Hi, how are you doing today? I was thinking about you." Just that little bit of an interaction would calm me down.

I don't remember when I made the decision to start going through his closet. I do remember that it wasn't easy. Certain clothing articles brought back memories. As I removed clothing from the closet, I would sort them in piles and sizes and think of who in the family might want to have them. I gave some to my brother, a couple of my nephews, and my dad. What they didn't want, I donated. I kept certain items in the closet. I wasn't ready to give them away yet. I would leave them there until I was mentally ready to do so.

Around May of 2010, I decided it was time to update my resume and put it online. I looked at a lot of job postings to help me figure out what type of position I wanted to pursue. After posting my resume on several job sites, I continued to look online for possible openings. In July I received a call from a career counselor asking me if I was interested in starting my own business. One of my dreams had been to do just that, but I never followed up on it and put it on the back burner. The counselor explained that he worked for franchise companies who were looking for individuals who had been in the corporate world for most of their career.

He saw my resume on one of the job sites and thought I would be a good candidate to purchase a franchise. I listened to what he had to say, and it got me thinking that this may be exactly what I needed.

I really didn't want to go back to the corporate world unless I had no other choice. After some thought I decided to initiate the discovery process to see what it was all about and whether it was right for me. He would be my career counselor and walk me through the process at no cost. He had me complete a DISC analysis, asked me a lot of questions as to what I liked to do and what I didn't. I told him that I had completed an interior design program at RISD and had a passion for decorating. After the skills analysis was finished, he recommended several different types of franchises. One of the choices was in interior decorating. I did my due diligence on all of them and decided to speak with two of the franchises and visit their corporate offices. I knew that this could be a risky endeavor and wasn't sure I was up for it. This would be completely opposite from my prior careers. After thinking about it, I decided that it couldn't hurt to visit both franchises and spend a couple of days at the corporate offices to learn as much as I could about what would be involved in becoming a franchisee. It was exciting and terrifying at the same time!

In August of 2010 I signed the paperwork and became a new franchisee for interior decorating! I was officially an entrepreneur starting a new business. This was going to be my passion career. Something that would make me happy as well as allow me to have more of a balance in my life. I was excited about the new path that I was pursuing and looking forward to meeting other franchisees. The franchise would provide me with the back-office support, vendor relationships, ongoing educational and sales training, and professional personal guidance that I needed in starting this new venture. I would not be alone in figuring out how to establish and run my company.

I joined a weekly networking group which enabled me to get back out there and meet new people and form new relationships. I felt overwhelmed and a bit scared about my new life venture, but I believed that it would help me to grow and expand my horizons and chart a new course. By putting myself out there, I learned a lot about myself. I could be strong and independent and create an active life for myself. No more of being the third wheel. I made new friends that I could socialize with both professionally and personally.

My new career kept me very busy and active. I didn't have time to sit around and be sad and feel sorry for myself. I had an opportunity to soar, explore new ideas, and help people. Helping people gave me a lot of satisfaction and a purpose. At times it was hard, and I questioned whether I did the right thing by changing careers, but I didn't give up.

I reminded myself that I had resources available to me with the franchise that would help me. I hated making mistakes and would get upset when I did. By reaching out I learned that it was okay to make mistakes if I learned from them. I didn't have to be perfect, and asking questions when I didn't know how to handle something was okay. I learned a lot and became a better person by allowing myself to admit that I didn't know the answer and asked someone to help me. It helped to reduce my stress levels.

I was used to going on a couple of vacations with Ron every year and I missed it. A close friend of mine knew how I felt and told me she would go with me if I felt up to it. I thought about it and decided to take her up on her offer. We went to Disneyworld. The last time I had been there it was with my husband. The trip taught me that it was okay to enjoy myself and have a good time with friends. I didn't have to feel guilty about it. He was still with me in my heart, and he would want me to go on and create new adventures.

Did I think about him while I was there? Of course I did. Did I wish that he was with me? Yes. I started to learn how to compartmentalize my feelings and not think of sad things and what might have been. I was still here, and I didn't want to be sad all the time. I gradually learned how to push the sadness away to a different place. You never forget what you've been through. Over time I was learning how to better manage my emotions and move forward. That didn't mean that I would no longer talk about him and keep everything in the past. I still get emotional at times, but it does get easier.

I learned that people don't know what to say when someone passes. People would constantly ask me if I would date again and possibly get married. I told them that that was the furthest thing from my mind at the moment. I was perfectly fine living on my own. This was not the time for that discussion. There were times when I felt lonely and thought it would be nice to have a male companion to go out to dinner or a movie with, but I didn't dwell on it. I believed if it was meant to happen, someday it would.

Going forward, my routine consisted of attending weekly networking meetings and occasional after-hours networking events. I interacted with a lot of people which provided me with the opportunity to make new friends and develop business relations with both males and females. I had a passion for my new business and wanted to share it with others. During this time, I met others who had lost a loved one. It gave me another outlet to express my feelings and what I was going through. The interactions were also helping me build my confidence and believe in myself.

Because my business is part of a franchise, I was provided with ongoing training, which included annual conferences and creating relationships with other decorators throughout the country. It provided me with the opportunity to form some lasting friendships, do some travelling, and grow as a person. I was on my way to creating a new path for myself. It was just what I needed.

I always loved spending time outdoors. During the summers I spent a lot of time with my family on weekends. We would get together at each other's homes and just hang out. We would have cookouts at my home and enjoy the day by the pool. I have lots of nieces and nephews, and I enjoyed watching them while they were in the pool. It warmed my heart.

It had been a while since I had played golf on a regular basis. I decided to join a women's golf league. It was an opportunity to have some fun and meet people with like interests. I had been part of other golf leagues, so I was familiar with how it worked. I needed to get back into the game and do something else besides the gym and work. The ladies were very welcoming, and I enjoyed the socialization as well as the golf. Since I owned my own business, I had the flexibility to play golf during the day. I met women who had lost their husbands too, and we could share stories. I am still part of that league today.

While attending my weekly networking meetings, I became friendly with a male acquaintance. One of the topics we discussed was the theatre. He was involved with a theatre company that was relocating to a new space. I enjoyed the theatre but hadn't gone to many shows. He happened to have an extra ticket for a show at Providence Performing Arts Center (PPAC) and wanted to know if I would like to go with him as friends. I wasn't sure if I wanted to go with him even though it wasn't a "date." He was the first guy that approached me about going out since Ron passed. My first thought was, *what will people think?* I quickly got over my insecurity and decided to take him up on his offer. There wasn't any reason why I shouldn't go. We liked each other's company, and he wasn't a stranger. On the day of the show, he picked me up. We were seeing a musical. After the performance, he took me out to dinner. It was an enjoyable experience, and I was glad I took him up on his offer.

A month or so later he asked me if I wanted to see another show with him. I accepted his invitation and had a good time. Gradually we got to know each other better and after a few months, he asked me to attend another show with him at a theatre that he enjoyed immensely. Because of him I had the opportunity to meet a lot of the actors that performed in the shows as well as the staff who ran the theatre. Eventually, I became his theatre buddy and saw many, many shows with him there as friends. I wasn't looking for a relationship and neither was he, but as time went on, we became closer friends and started a relationship. It was nice to have someone to be with and enjoy myself.

He asked me to go on vacation with him to Mexico. After some thought I accepted his invitation. I had never traveled to Mexico, so I was excited to go. It felt a little awkward at first, but I was eager to experience something new and get out of my comfort zone. It ended up being a very enjoyable trip and much needed vacation. When we got back to the states, we continued to see each other. I didn't expect to get involved in a relationship with him. We were very different. I was willing to try and I'm glad I took the chance. We spent a lot of time together and continued to have an enjoyable time.

We ended up vacationing together once a year to Mexico. At times our relationship was challenging but we learned to compromise and work through our differences. As a result, our relationship continued to grow. We're not perfect but the relationship works for us. We have our ups and downs, but because we value each other and respect each other's feelings we can work through issues or differences of opinion in a positive way. He's an important part of my life and I look forward to our future together. It's been nine years since we first met.

My journey taught me that it was possible to create a new life with someone else. I learned that it was okay to move on and feel good about my life again. I no longer feel guilty about moving on. I believe that Ron would want me to be happy again. I believe that I deserve to make the most of my life. That doesn't mean that I don't think about him or talk about him. I will forever have our memories and will never forgot what I went through. It will always be a part of me. I'm in a different place now, and I try not to take anything for granted. Little things don't bother me like they used to. I allowed myself to have a new perspective on life. I try to live for today and enjoy the moment. We don't know how much time we have in this world so if there's something that you really want to do, go for it! Don't keep postponing it. It's not always easy, but it's well worth the journey. I am a survivor and a strong and independent person. You can be that person, too, if you give yourself permission. I did!

CHAPTER 7

The Hard Way

*In loving memory of
Arthur Gott—May 11, 1930 to February 14, 2005,
David Gott—February 14, 1965 to October 9, 2008, and
Lisa Horne—May 17, 1971 to February 21, 2017*

by Catherine DeOrsey

Valentine's Day 2005 will always have a piece of my heart. It's not the day I got a beautiful necklace or the day I went away on a surprise romantic getaway. It also wasn't the day I dressed my adorable three-month baby girl in a Valentine-inspired outfit covered with little hearts. This is the commercial picture of Valentine's Day. For me, this is the day I held my father's hand and watched him struggle to take his last breath of life. Although seventeen years have passed, I can remember it like it was yesterday. This was the first time I lost someone I loved. Then, years later, I lost my brother and my friend.

I wasn't prepared for the toll grief would take on my life. No one ever talked to me about grief. I had no idea what grief was and didn't understand there's a process to go through after you bury the person you love. I thought it was over when the person died. I thought you did your best to get back to the life you were living before. Of course, somedays were good and some days were bad, but I thought, *that's just how life is.* I learned the hard way that grief is a powerful emotion that must be processed and released. If not, it will come back at some point in time, in some form or another, and force you to reconcile it. To heal from grief takes more than what I did. I want you to process your grief. I want you to process it in a way that is gentle to you and prevents you from learning what I did the hard way.

In 2004, when my father got sick, it seemed like it came out of nowhere. I was three months pregnant with my first child after mis-carrying the year before. My father was at work when he felt a pain in his side and left early to go see his doctor. His doctor told him, "There's two small dots on your lung," and immediately started treating him for pneumonia. A few weeks later, he still wasn't better and suddenly those "two little dots" turned into something "more."

I remember the day like it was yesterday. I called my parents on the drive home from work. My father told me he just saw the nurses and they assured him, "Mr. Gott, you're going to be fine!" As soon as I got home and walked up the front stairs my husband flew open the door and said, "You need to call your father." Little did I know when I hung up the phone earlier, my father got a call to go see his doctor. What started out as "two little dots" just a few weeks earlier morphed into "You have stage four small cell lung cancer. It's in the lymph nodes. There's nothing we can do. You have six-to-nine months to live."

I couldn't believe what I just heard. Being pregnant I immediately wondered if he would even be here to meet my first child. To say I was in shock was an understatement. The plan was for him to start chemo and radiation in three days. I had no idea what to expect with all this. This was my first time witnessing someone go through cancer and all that it entails.

The internal pain I was feeling was like nothing I felt before. As I grappled with the news of losing my father, I thought about ways to stay busy and "happy." Instinctively, I didn't want to feel this pain and the barrage of heavy emotions that arrived. Throughout this journey, I was in constant contact with my brothers and parents but looking back, we didn't talk about our emotions and how each of us were feeling. I didn't talk about it with my husband either. I didn't talk about how I was feeling to anyone. I kept those feelings inside and focused on my pregnancy and work while keeping up with my father's status and needs.

Grief's pain is so intense, it's no wonder I tried to block and ignore it. I now know this is a typical and natural response to pain that serves as a protective mechanism so one doesn't fall apart. My mother's instinct was to protect my unborn child so I focused on keeping myself strong so I could deliver a happy, healthy baby in the coming months. The way I responded to grief seemed like a good idea at the time, but little did I know this avoidance approach would have tremendous consequences to my health twelve years later.

Once the chemo and radiation started, my father was sick for the next eight and a half months of his life. He didn't live those months. He suffered from nausea and vomiting, dizziness, weight loss and hair loss, and burning of his throat. Although I worked for the pharmaceutical industry, I was clearly naïve. I didn't know medications could come with such consequences to one's quality of life. In my narrow view, I thought these treatments were only supposed to help. I got to witness the side effects firsthand while sitting next to my father one night at dinner. Since my father's cancer was in his lung, the radiation treatment burned his throat. It was so uncomfortable to watch my father eat. With every bite he winced and struggled as he tried to swallow his food in pain. I hated watching my father like this. I tried to focus on eating dinner but kept staring at him out of the corner of my eye. Suddenly, I lost my appetite.

At this point, six months had passed, and my father's health was going downhill. I knew my father didn't have much time. I wanted to make sure I told him I loved him and thanked him for being a great father. Since we didn't communicate our feelings, I thought by writing a "goodbye" letter, it would keep me focused and ensure I got out everything I wanted to say. The thought of doing this was tough. I couldn't believe I was even in the situation to have to consider this. One thing was writing it, the other thing was reading it. I wanted my father to hear how I felt from my voice rather than reading the words on paper. I was so nervous to read this letter which is strange because I had a great relationship with my father. I never knew saying simple words like "I love you," "thank you," and "goodbye" would feel the way it did. I guess that's what happens when you don't communicate your feelings for someone you love and then are forced to tell them when they are on their death bed. I knew I needed to do this so I wouldn't live with regret. I faced my fears and started to write.

Saying the final goodbye to someone you love that's dying is one of the worst things I've ever had to do. While my father laid on the couch, I started to read the letter. I told him how much I loved him. I thanked him for all the things he did for me. I told him he was a great father. I reminded him of all the funny stories of our family and told him these were things that I would never forget. I remember I was crying and sweating with each word and sentence that I read. My father's reaction was quiet. He didn't say a word as he listened and smiled but it was the look on his face that I most remember. I knew my father was listening, but he was also somewhere else. I could see it. My father had one foot in this world, and one foot in the other. His transition had already started. He was getting ready to leave this world. It was in that moment that I had a final realization. This letter that I was so stressed and worried about writing and reading was never for him all along. The letter was for me. He didn't need it. He already knew how I felt.

This letter became a vehicle for me to say everything I wanted so I wouldn't live with regret. Living with grief is hard enough but living with regret on top of it is another. Regret is torture to one's soul. It is another one of those invisible, painful emotions like grief that will wreak havoc on your insides if it is not processed. As difficult as the experience was, I'm so grateful I had the opportunity to do it. I'm grateful I faced my fears. I'm grateful I was given the gift of time. Not everybody gets that chance.

I have no doubt that writing that letter helped me through my healing journey. Another huge blessing that got me through this time was when my sweet baby girl, Daniella, arrived on November 15, 2004! I thanked God so many times for giving me this needed light and love. I thanked God I have pictures when my father came to the hospital to see me and his new granddaughter! I needed that and I didn't even know it. There were so many unforgettable precious newborn moments that picked up my spirit and allowed me to continue. Having my daughter gave me something to smile about. I have no idea how I would have gotten through the grief of losing my father without having Daniella. For someone so small, she had no idea how much she was helping me by being born at that time. It's strange to see how life happens sometimes. As one life ends, another one begins. Now that I've been through it, I can see divine's perfect timing and now know there's always a plan behind the plan. In the midst of our suffering, we might not feel it, but I have learned and believe we are never alone.

Thank God we're not alone because unbeknownst to me, Valentine's

Day Weekend would become one of the most traumatic events of my life and greatest source of so much pain. It was now February 12, and I decided to take Daniella for a visit to see my father. As soon as I opened the front door and walked through the kitchen, everyone in my house was crying. I put Daniella's car seat down and ran down the hallway to see what was going on in my parents' bedroom.

There was my father laying on his bed. His eyes were closed, and he was struggling to breathe. It felt like someone turned on a light switch. Yesterday I talked to him and today he couldn't talk or breathe. My mom was holding his hand while my brothers and I gathered on his bed. The tears flowed down my face as I grabbed his other hand. I didn't want to look at his face, so I watched and listened to his slow, congested breaths out of the corner of my eye. With each inhale and exhale, we were holding onto dear life wondering if it was going to be the last. Each breathe got longer and deeper. They had this sound I never heard before. This was the first time I heard the sound of death. This went on for a few minutes and then he quieted down. Suddenly, he was resting in what appeared to be a coma-like state and then nothing happened.

I didn't know what was going on since this was the first time I witnessed someone die. I thought it was going to happen right then and there. I guess it wasn't his time so my brothers and I decided to leave the room so he could rest and be with my mom. I can't imagine how my parents were feeling throughout this journey with grief. After all, they had been happily married for forty-three years.

I sat in the living room and bounced Daniella on my lap while my brothers small talked with my aunt and uncle. While my father lay in a coma-like state, I heard out of the corner of my ear, "David, David, are you okay?" I immediately turned my head, and my brother was in the middle of the living room floor convulsing and flailing his arms. I jumped up and gave my daughter to my aunt and ran to call 911. My brother Rob stayed with David to see if he needed CPR.

As I hung up with 911, my mother started walking down the hall. I thought to myself, *nooooooooo—she can't see this*! I immediately turned her around from seeing David. I said, "Mom, go back to Dad. Something's wrong with David. 911 is on the way." There was no way she could handle seeing David like this. My father was already dying and if David died too, she was going to have a heart attack and die from all the stress.

911 came and took David away. My brothers and I just looked at each other in disbelief. *What the hell just happened?* was all I could think. With David at the hospital and my father "stable," I closed my eyes and my mind spun with questions: *What's wrong with David? Is he going to die? Now? At the same time as my father? What about Dad? When is he going to die? How is this going to happen? What's death going to sound like?*

It was close to eleven at night when the hospital finally called. They told us, "It's just stress. David signed himself out, and he's already on his way home." I couldn't believe they didn't keep him overnight because the stress in our house was only going to get worse. It was almost midnight when David walked through the door. We sat in the living room and told him we loved him. We talked with him about his fears and his worries. He was worried my father was going to die on his birthday, Valentine's Day, which was fast approaching. He also was filled with his own regret and pain as his relationship with my father and our family was strained due to his struggle with addiction and mental health issues. He had been kicked out of the house many times while my father was battling cancer, and now that he was in the house, he was trying to behave. This meant he wasn't getting his daily normal daily "fix" that, unfortunately, his body now needed. All of this combined added to the burden of the situation.

After our family intervention, we finally got off to bed. I was sleeping in the basement with my husband and daughter when suddenly I heard a loud thump at 2:30 a.m.. I immediately ran upstairs to see what happened now. I ran down the hallway and looked in my father's bedroom. The thump didn't come from him. I opened the door to David's bedroom and there he was laying on the floor. He had fallen out of bed and didn't look good. I asked him his name, date of birth, and if he knew where he was. He was disoriented and had no idea. I ran down the hall to call 911 again! It hadn't even been three hours since David was home. I kept wondering what the neighbors were thinking. Each time 911 arrived, they were coming for my brother, not my father. What was happening was so unimaginable. I felt like it was something you would see on Oprah except that it was happening to us!

The morning came and the hospital called. This time they finally told us the truth. What happened to David wasn't just stress. For the first time in his struggle with addiction, his body was reacting because he wasn't getting his fix. While I held Daniella waiting for my father to die, my brother had a full-blown seizure right in front of our eyes. Addiction had him. His body now needed alcohol and opioids to function "normally." This brought the severity of his addiction to a whole new level for me. I didn't know this could happen. I didn't know much about addiction at the time. The only thing I knew was what it did to my brother and our family, and I hated it.

It was now Valentine's Day. David was home after being released from the hospital. Finally, after two long days of being in a coma-like state, my father's breathing started to change. It sounded like he was holding onto a cliff. He would inhale slowly and then hold on. Eventually, the air would fall out of his lips. This was it. Hospice told us so.

Thankfully, divine's timing was perfect. David was home so we could all say good-bye. We crowded around my father's bed so he wasn't alone. He kept holding on, he wouldn't let go. The room was silent. You could hear a pin drop. Listening to those breaths was killing me. I knew it was his time to go and somebody needed to say something. Eventually, I took my father's hand, and I told him he had to go. I told him to look for the white light and it was okay for him to leave. I told him, "We will be okay, it's time." It took a few minutes, but finally and eventually, my father stopped struggling to breathe. That was it. My father was gone. He died on Valentine's Day, David's Birthday, 2005.

Seventeen years have passed, and I still can't believe what happened that weekend. My father's battle with cancer took a nosedive on Friday, February 12. He could have died on the twelfth, thirteenth, fifteenth, or any other day, but nope, Valentine's Day and David's birthday it was. I can't tell you how many times I've replayed the story of that weekend inside my mind. I had no idea what I was doing to myself every time I did that. I couldn't seem to get it out of my head.

Once my father was gone, I picked up my life and focused on my family and work. The pain of losing my father came and went, especially on birthdays and holidays. I really felt it when I went home to visit Mom. It felt weird not seeing him sitting in his chair watching movies or the Red Sox. I hated not being able to see his face and give him a hug. I tried to keep Mom busy and give her something to smile about with Daniella. My father never flew so I took her on a needed vacation to Hawaii to pick our spirits up. I'm so grateful we had that memory together. We had so many laughs we still talk about today, and we felt Dad's presence right there with us!

Facing Valentine's Day weekend was tough for many years. This day had such a sore spot in my heart and the day felt awkward. I tried to smile and be "up" when someone said, "Happy Valentine's Day," but my heart just wasn't into it. My husband didn't know what to do for me on this day. The reality was there was nothing he or anyone could do to make things better. Eventually, I realized the only one that could make this day better for me was me. If I wanted to feel better, I had to make a choice to accept what happened and let go of that story. I needed to make the most of that day for my children and my husband. I did my best to move forward and loosen the grip "that weekend" had on my mind for so long.

My mom and I talked a lot about that day since the loss of my father. Over time, we decided we needed to look at it differently. Since Valentine's Day is the day of love, we chose to see the love in the day. Since God is love and God loves his children, perhaps he chose to take my father on that day to take away his suffering as a sign of his love. From now on, my father is living in peace and love. With this newfound perspective, it eased the pain. I focused my attention on the love for my family, father, and brother. It was David's birthday after all! I focused on trying to help Mom smile. This new way of thinking wasn't an easy habit to create. It felt forced in the beginning, but I smiled through it. I stuck with it and practiced a "love" approach each year.

Over time, the story slowed down in my mind and eventually I was able to smile more. The less I thought about it, the better I started to feel. Today, on Valentine's Day, I start and end the day with a quiet "I love you, Dad and David" and a few times in-between. I have learned this new approach is a needed form of self-care that has tremendous value on my overall health and well-being. Every time I practice thinking this new way of being, I give my mind a needed break and it fills my body, mind, and spirit with the greatest form of healing energy, called LOVE!

The next three years were busy with life: two kids, a dog and home, and two working parents. Out of nowhere my phone rang one morning at 5 a.m. I was in a sound sleep, but quickly picked it up and ran to the hallway to not wake up my husband. It was my mom. She said, "Catherine, are you up? David's dead."

It was October 9, 2008, and my brother finally lost his battle with addiction. Grief had arrived the second time. I slumped on the stairs half-awake with the phone in my ear trying to process what I just heard. At seventy years old, my mom went downstairs to let her dog out. She found her son, my brother, blue and dead on the floor at forty-three years of age. While this wasn't necessarily a surprise, I wasn't ready for the call that morning.

Losing my brother was my second experience with grief but it felt different this time. It was because of the way he died. My brother died from a fatal overdose. The autopsy report came back with the cause of death due to opioids, alcohol, and cocaine. I didn't expect to hear cocaine was in his system. This news stung me to my core. I should have been sad, but the truth is I was angry. I was mad at my brother. I sat in awe and shook my head. I said to my mother, "He did this to himself."

I'm not proud of how I responded to my brother's death. I know it sounds bad. The truth is I was naïve and didn't understand addiction. I knew my brother had a drinking problem, but I didn't know he was addicted. I didn't know he had a disease which is better known today as Substance Abuse Disorder.

Because of exhaustion, embarrassment, and a desire to keep things private, my mom wanted to keep the funeral small. Deep down, because I was also angry, I didn't even want to invite my friends. I was naïve and judgmental. I didn't know what I didn't know. Everyone in town knew my brother had a problem and knew how he died. I'm ashamed to admit it but I didn't even reach out to my friends to let them know. One friend heard it from another and showed up at the funeral. I ended up telling my other friends when I saw them four months later. Unfortunately, this is what the stigma of addiction does. It takes everything from you.

I didn't know how to handle David's death. I didn't know what to do because of how he died. I now know that shouldn't have mattered, but I didn't know that then. For twenty years, I lived with the roller coaster ride of my brother's addiction. The harsh truth is, I was sick of all the drama. I was tired of worrying about him and my parents. I was tired of the lies and exhausted from it all. I wanted to get through the funeral and put it all behind me. I wanted to move on as quickly as I could. Once again, I thought I could ignore the pain of losing someone I love. I returned to work and continued moving forward. No therapy, no rest, no self-care. I again focused on family and work and the next three years were full of life. Life was busy but it was a good busy!

David was gone which meant the addiction was gone. Life was quieter after David passed but it doesn't mean you don't miss the person you lost. Someone you love shouldn't need to die for you to get peace in your life but that's the sad reality of what happened. Addiction comes with a cost to everyone as well as a stigma, but it doesn't mean that stigma is right. If David had only gotten the real help he needed to bring balance to his body, mind, and spirit, then David and our family wouldn't have suffered as much.

It was now about 2013, three to four years since David passed. I travelled a lot for work, so I had plenty of long windshield time in my car or on a plane. One night while driving home late from New York City, it finally hit me that I lost my *brother*. Out of nowhere, I broke down crying. This was the first time I really cried for losing my brother. I cried out to David and told him I was sorry. I was sorry for being mad and that I couldn't help him. I was sorry he died the way he did and wished he got the help he needed and deserved. This was the first time I grieved for my brother, and it took three to four years after his death for me to experience it. I learned that grief didn't die when David died. I unconsciously squished grief down for years within myself until grief decided it was time for me to release its contents from my body, mind, and spirit.

About seven years later, I broke down again. It was 2019 and I was attending a "coincidental" meeting on the opioid crisis. At this meeting, this was the first time in ten years that I ever equated my brother's death to the opioid crisis. Because of my experience with addiction and desire to prevent this, I ended up creating an innovative non-profit to help community members get well, stay well, and be well. I finally felt I was doing something positive with David's story and felt he was guiding me through the journey. It was hard being back in the addiction space at times. There are so many families that had and have it worse off than me and are still living with the fear, anxiety, worry, stress, and grief that I was once filled with. However, I know doing something positive with my grief to help other people has played a tremendous role in my healing today.

At this point I thought I'd fully processed my grief. However, one weekend while writing this chapter my stomach started to hurt and the floodgates opened up again. This time it was all because of David. Writing this chapter, I cried endless tears of sorrow about everything that happened. I cried to David again. I forgave myself for what I did and didn't do for my brother. I forgave myself for what I didn't know. While I knew reliving and sharing my story would be tough, I didn't expect to have such a strong emotional reaction, especially since I lost my brother fifteen years ago. I am still learning about grief. Grief is a much more powerful emotion than I ever realized. It's taken me a LONG time to learn this lesson.

I finally learned about grief the hard way when I was faced with it again in 2017. No one should ever have to hand the phone to a nine-year-old little boy so he can learn his mom just died. That's what I had to do when I lost my friend, Lisa, on February 21, 2017. While all my losses have been painful, this experience was excruciating for me because I gave my whole self to Lisa's situation. I was so intimately connected in my body, mind, and spirit. The strange thing was I didn't know Lisa and her family that long and we weren't the best of friends yet. Our family friendship was developing quickly but we clearly had a connection. This situation rocked me, and I was on a mission to try to prevent her from dying.

Lisa was young and healthy when her back started hurting. I remember dropping my son off at her house when her husband jokingly said, "Be careful when you turn forty-five, everything starts to fall apart." Little did we all know, she only had seven months to live.

2016 was supposed to be an amazing summer. I had the entire summer off for the first time ever. I planned a cruise to Alaska, to be more present with my family, and to get some needed rest and relaxation! I never expected to endure what happened next.

One day while at a kids' birthday party, Lisa told me her back was hurting. This was unusual as she took care of herself. She didn't fall or have an accident either. A few weeks went by and the pain was still there, so her doctor ordered an MRI. The news came back that they saw "something," and they thought it could be something like leukemia. I could see the worry in their eyes.

At that time, I worked for the number one oncology biotech company. I was connected to some of the best medications for cancer and had numerous ways to get in touch with the top oncologists across the country. If you have to come down with cancer, at least I was connected to help. I dove right in headfirst to quickly get her the best care I could find. While they waited for test results, we carpooled our boys back and forth to basketball camp. That week was like someone switched on a light switch with this cancer. One day Lisa was driving the boys to camp, the next day she had trouble taking one small step out her front door. She started to speak, and her mouth was off to the side.

"Lisa, what's wrong?" I asked.

"They think it's benign cysts," she said in excruciating pain and fear. I didn't know what this was, but this was not good.

On Friday night, I was headed to Boston with my family for an early morning flight to start our cruise to Alaska. I planned to drive the boys that day and keep them with me while Lisa and Don got her test results. It was 3:30 p.m. when Don gave me a call. It wasn't good. I asked him to share the results so I could get them to the right oncologist ASAP. I hadn't even started packing yet when I downloaded her tests. I knew what I was reading given my medical background. As I read her report and shook my head in disbelief, tears came to my eyes as I stared at her nine-year-old son in my kitchen and thought about Maya, her eleven-year-old daughter. I was sick to my stomach. My kids were the same ages. This was a nightmare.

While Alaska was amazing, it was bittersweet. I was literally sick to my stomach a lot and was clearly a mess a few times. My husband told me I had to stop thinking about it and have a good time. I was determined to do my best to enjoy. I would figure something out to help when I came home.

Now the journey with oncologists, cancer treatments, and clinical trials had arrived. While there's no doubt this experience took a toll on me, there were also some beautiful bittersweet moments that changed my life forever. I learned some of my greatest lessons with grief going through this experience.

One beautiful moment happened when I got to make an unexpected visit with Lisa during her fifty-four-day hospital stay in isolation. How I even got in to see her was a miracle on its own. To protect Lisa from infection, her husband was the only person allowed to be with her. Not even her kids or her two sisters. One day while driving I had this very heavy burden that I needed to visit her. This was not coming from me as I knew I would never do anything to jeopardize her health. This was coming from a divine source and its nudging wouldn't stop. I didn't know what to do and why it was happening but what if Lisa could get a miracle? I would've done anything to save her, so I put my fears aside and called her husband so I didn't live in regret.

Don knew I was shaken, and this was more than me. He knew I'd be careful, so he opened the door and allowed me to follow through on the nudge I was being given. I was nervously relieved and on my way to the hospital when the phone rang a few minutes later. It was Lisa and she was not happy I was coming. Her throat hurt. She was in pain, couldn't eat, and didn't want visitors. She was angry.

She tried hard to block me. Ordinarily, if a dying person asked me not to do something, I would listen. I started crying when I told her what happened. I told her I thought God wanted me to sit with her and touch her for some unknown reason. I didn't know why this was happening and this had never happened to me before. Something inside told me I needed to be there that day. She reluctantly agreed and as soon as I hung up the phone, I couldn't believe what happened. My radio flew on (it was off), and the song and verse that was on was Sam Smith, "I just want to be by your side to make sure you're all right." This was exactly what I just told her I felt God wanted me to do! This had to be a sign of a miracle. I hoped and prayed!

When I got to her room, I couldn't believe what I saw. Here was my friend, a beautiful, healthy forty-five-year-old human being fighting for her life right in front of my eyes. She looked nothing like her old self. I witnessed the shocking transformation of what a few weeks of aggressive cancer, chemo, and radiation can do to a person.

The nutritionist came in to talk with Lisa. Lisa was not happy with her or the food. I got to witness the patient tell the nutritionist that the yogurt she ate at home was better than what the hospital gave her when she had cancer. She went on to educate her that she prefered organic and hers was made with better ingredients than the crap they served in the hospital. I couldn't help but look away and silently smirk as I listened to Lisa reem her a new one. It wasn't the nutritionist's fault. It was the fault of our healthcare system. Either way, Lisa was right, and someone needed to hear about it.

As soon as she left, Lisa told me her story. She cried, telling me everything she'd been through. She talked about everything that the community had done for her and her family. She eventually said, "This is the best thing that ever happened to me. There has been so much love." I literally sat there in awe. There I was looking at my friend: she was only forty-five years old, had been in isolation for thirty-plus days, her hair was all over the pillow, she had lost SO much weight, and she was saying this was the best thing that ever happened to her. This had changed Lisa. She was now awake.

I have no doubt this is the reason God pushed me to be with Lisa that day. God wanted me to witness something, to share the message of love with other people. Love shows itself in the darkest of places and transcends pain and suffering. Through her cancer diagnosis, Lisa was connecting to the source of love more than she ever had before. As a result, she was now seeing love more than she ever had before. People in the community, including my family and I, were responding with more love than they typically did.

Love was with Lisa and her family right in the middle of their worst nightmare. It showed itself to be seen and felt to bring peace and love to those who needed it. WOW! To top it off, I stopped by to see her husband on my way home. He talked about how he drove to the hospital every day and what he went through. He said on his way in to see Lisa each day he wondered "how something so painful can be so beautiful." WHAT? Did he now just say what Lisa said earlier? WOW. Love and God were with Don too. While I hoped to get a miracle that day, I got a lasting message to share with people in the midst of their suffering. Something greater was happening that day. This is one of the greatest lessons and gifts I have ever received.

Ultimately, weeks went on and Lisa's cancer wasn't responding. Dana Faber said there was nothing else they could do but she could try to get into a clinical trial. Almost all the clinical trials were closed and not accepting new patients. Thankfully, I was able to leverage my connections and get Lisa an expedited appointment at The University of Pennsylvania for the highly anticipated Car-T Cell Clinical Trial. The doctor told Don and Lisa he had ten people in his waiting room and only six openings. Ugh. He also told them that she was the youngest and worst patient he would have and didn't know if she would make it through the trial. Despite that, he surprisingly decided to accept her in the trial. Unbelievable. Against all odds, we just got a miracle! That immediately flooded us all with hope. We needed that.

Lisa started the Car-T Cell Trial a few short weeks later. The doctors removed all her t-cells which are one of the important white blood cells that are critically important for the immune system to function properly. She would be at high risk for infection while waiting at home for doctors to make her new t-cells. They planned to go back a few weeks later to receive her new cells and wait for her cancer to respond. One day while Lisa was at home, her vision started to go blurry along with new headaches. This meant her cancer was still spreading and now it was in her brain. This was it. Lisa was done. She was exhausted and tired of fighting. Despite the love for her husband, kids, and family, she was ready to move on with her soul's journey.

Charlie, her son, was with us for most of the summer. He slept over the night he learned what hospice was. He was with us a few nights later when I handed him the phone to talk to his dad to learn his mom just died. As a mom with two kids of both the same young age, words cannot express how excruciating this was for me. Charlie was so cute. Both her kids were. I loved them like they were my own. I loved Lisa and I loved this family. They were good people. What were these kids going to do without their mom? I felt their pain every step of the way. I tried to stop this from happening with everything I could. I held on as tight as I could, but Lisa ran out of time. Ultimately, we were too late.

For seven months, I worried about this. I worried about everything: Lisa, her husband and kids, and her sisters. I used to sit on my front porch and think about how someone young and healthy gets picked out of the sky and dies a few months later. It didn't make sense. I've learned behind all that worry, I was living in constant fear. I was afraid of the pain of losing my friend and afraid of Don and the kids being alone. Because of my fear, I tried to control the situation doing everything I could to save her. I didn't take care of my body, mind, and spirit, and eventually this took a toll on me. Little did I know, God was in control. God was with us. There was a plan behind the plan.

Life continued to move forward after Lisa's passing. Eventually, Don met this amazing woman named Julie-Ann and they married two years later. While some people might have struggled with meeting someone new, I have no doubt this was purposely orchestrated by Lisa and the divine. Here was this beautiful woman that was single and had needs of her own. She was beautiful on the outside and full of love and energy on the inside but lived with the pain of never being able to have kids. Little did she know at the perfect time she'd meet this man with two kids in need of her love. God's plan always has a purpose and comes at the perfect time. I needed to learn to surrender my fears and worries to God and trust that everything would be okay as it surely was.

It was no small feat for Julie-Ann to walk into this heart-breaking situation. Lisa was known and loved by many, but God and Lisa knew what they were doing when they chose Julie-Ann. At Don and Julie-Ann's wedding, I got to witness many beautiful things: how Julie-Ann gracefully and intentionally incorporated Lisa into their wedding and how Lisa's sisters joined hands and genuinely smiled with Julie-Ann for pictures. I also got to watch Charlie cry his eyes out talking about both his mom and Julie-Ann while giving the best man's speech at their wedding. To this day, all these memories consume me with tears of bittersweet joy.

Love and Lisa are all around this family and it's the most beautiful thing that I've ever seen. After all my worries and fears, there was never anything I had to worry about. God was in control, like always, and had a plan for Lisa and her family as well as for Julie-Ann. Julie-Ann and I have a special connection too. I've told her while I love Lisa and did everything I could to save her, I didn't lose a friend, I gained another. For some reason, Lisa and I weren't meant to have a long earthly friendship, but I was there when she needed me most. Julie-Ann is a blessing in people's lives and I'm grateful I can continue a close relationship with my new friend.

I learned the hard way that everything will always be okay despite the way it looks or feels especially in the beginning. There's always a plan behind the plan and had I known then what I know now, I could have saved myself a ton of pain. My greatest and final lesson has been that I must take care of myself and put myself first. I must take care of my body, mind, and spirit if I want to get well, stay well, and be well. It took me getting diagnosed with severe Crohn's Disease to realize I must take care of myself.

In the background of Lisa battling her cancer, my stomach started to hurt. After three days of stomach pain, I drove myself to the emergency room thinking it was my appendix. I sat alone in a quiet room waiting for test results from my doctor. In the midst of my pain and suffering, I heard a voice from somewhere say, "It's not what you think it is." My doctor walked in and said, "Who in your family has Crohn's Disease? You have severe Crohn's Disease with multiple ulcers, a fistula, an abscess, and so much inflammation, we can't even get a pediatric scope through your intestines. You need to be on a biologic medication right away."

I couldn't believe what I was hearing. No one in my family had Crohn's Disease. Because of where I worked, I knew what all this meant. This wasn't good. Now Lisa and I were patients together. My mind was spinning. How was this happening? Who was that voice? And by the way, that voice was right! It wasn't what I thought it was. I thought it was my appendix. How did this happen out of nowhere? Or…did it?

It took me two years from being admitted to the hospital to figure out this diagnosis didn't come out of nowhere. My husband told me, "You got sick because of what happened to Lisa." I learned it wasn't Lisa's situation that made me sick. Lisa's cancer and that entire experience was the final straw though. I realized in that moment that I lived with thirty years of chronic stress and grief and never took care of myself. I put myself last my entire life and eventually I broke. This is why I got sick.

I spent the next three nights in the hospital mortified about what I witnessed as a patient. This was my first time being on the other side of healthcare. That's a book for another day! I was on two IV antibiotics to help with pain and inflammation while doctors tried to decide if I needed surgery. The days were long. To keep myself busy, I meditated and listened to my certain music. Three days I was in the hospital and three times I heard "that voice" say "You will be healed." Hmm. I don't know why this kept happening, but I loved that message! My husband and kids looked worriedly at me in the hospital bed. My son asked if I had cancer like Lisa. I told them no and looked at my husband. I told him I heard, "I will be healed." I honestly wasn't worried about me anymore. I kept hearing these messages and felt it inside. I was so confident I was going to be healed that I secretly cancelled my appointment for the medication the doctors insisted I needed.

Little did I know, God had another plan for my healing journey. Despite my gut intuition and God's messages, the pain came back two weeks later. Ugh. I thought I was going to be healed right away. This situation was testing me. It was challenging everything I ever thought, believed, and knew to be true. I asked my doctors in the hospital how this happened. They told me that Crohn's Disease was an autoimmune condition, that they didn't know why it happens. The body just attacks itself. They said, "It's something you must live with for the rest of your life, but not to worry because there's miracle drugs for it."

For some surprising reason, I didn't want to be on these medications even though I knew they could help. I asked if there were other options and was told there were none. None of this sounded right to me. I never expected to not be aligned with my doctors. I always had been every time before. For some reason, deep down inside, this didn't make sense. My mind was spinning again. How could there really be no other options? I didn't want to be sick and live on these medications for the rest of my life. The pain was bad. I had no choice but to accept the situation despite what I thought was right and what I thought God wanted me to do. I wasn't happy about this and honestly, was confused.

I couldn't believe this was happening and how bad off I was. I thought I had been taking care of myself by working out and eating pretty good. I was known for being healthy. I've since learned my definition of health only addressed my physical nature. Throughout my life, I paid no attention to my mental, emotional, and spiritual well-being besides going to church. Clearly, what I was doing wasn't enough to take care of my needs.

The medication I needed was given through an IV and took five hours to receive every eight weeks. I was in a room with patients with cancer amongst other diseases like rheumatoid arthritis. Coincidentally, I used to sell and represent these medications working for the pharmaceutical/biotech industry. Now I was the patient. I never expected this, but I hated being on this medication. Without thinking I constantly found myself saying, "This is so stupid, I don't even know why I'm doing this. This drug isn't even working." And guess what? At the end of one year of being on this medication, my doctor did a colonoscopy and told me it didn't work! The number one product for fistulizing Crohn's Disease had zero impact on the inflammation in my body. The only thing it did do was cause my liver to have side effects which was the last thing I needed given everything else that was going on.

I was at a crossroads in my life. I just wasted a year of my life, and my condition was no better. In fact it was worse. My insurance company spent $171,000 that year on my care for a drug that didn't even work and caused side effects! This was unbelievable to me especially given where I worked. My doctor told me I had two choices: increase the dose of that drug or switch to a different medication. I asked about the side effects and if there was a potential risk for developing lymphoma like the other one. He said, "No. There is a potential, very rare side effect but it's never happened on this drug. I'm mentioning it because it's happened on similar medications. It's called PML." I couldn't believe what he just said. I knew what PML was because I worked for the biotech industry.

PML stands for Progressive Multifocal Leukoencephalopathy, or in common terms, it's a fatal brain disease. This immediately brought up old memories. I told him that I was not his average patient, and I knew what this meant. I told him I lost my job because three patients came down with PML from the drug I was representing. The company did the right thing and removed the drug from the market. As a result, we all lost our jobs. Those three poor patients and their families were going to suffer the pain of grief one day because of a drug I represented.

With this information, I didn't know what I was going to do, but for some reason I felt like I was being protected. Although I knew the risk of these side effects are very rare, rare is still real when it happens to you or to someone you love. I knew there was no way I could recover from a fatal brain disease, and I didn't feel like potentially coming down with lymphoma. Also, coincidentally, three months before I got sick, my brother called me because someone at his work had a fifteen-year-old son with Crohn's Disease and was doing great on this drug I used to sell. However, the boy ended up coming down with stage four lymphoma from the drug. I spoke to his father before I got sick. Looking back, it's crazy how the Universe was protecting me the entire time.

I didn't want any of this. I didn't want to be sick or on these medications. I truly believed that somehow, I would be healed. There HAD to be another way and I guess it was up to me to try and figure this thing out! While I was on a mission to try to save Lisa, I was also on a mission to find other treatment options for me. Most of all, I wanted to know why this happened in the first place so I could heal and prevent it from ever happening again. This was the start of my healing journey, and little did I know I'd be sharing my learnings to help all of you down the road!

I started researching everything I could find about Crohn's Disease: what it really is, treatment options, and reading patient stories from those that have been living with the disease. I was consumed and laser focused on my mission. I still hadn't decided what I was going to do next. My mind was on overload, so I decided to pause. I stepped away from my research and finally asked myself, *what is the main problem in my condition?* I kept reviewing all my tests and labs and gave myself the space I needed. I finally could see the biggest issue I had. I had massive amounts of inflammation in my body.

From there, I stopped labeling it Crohn's Disease and focused my research on inflammation: what is it, how it's created, and how it's treated. Wow! This approach opened a whole new world for me. I was onto something, I felt it. Of course, I knew what inflammation was but only from a physical perspective given my background (I was also a physical therapist).

However, because I was in crisis mode, I was open to learning anything new I could find. I learned that inflammation is created not just from a trauma or injury but also from chemicals in our food, environmental toxins that we put in our homes, alcohol, and sugar, as well as chemicals in our cleaning, skincare, and beauty products. I also learned inflammation can be created from the continuous thoughts and emotions from our mind! Wow. I found this all to be so interesting and it made total sense. I never knew any of this. Now this made me wonder what might have caused Dad and Lisa's cancer. I had so many questions.

From here many "coincidences" started to occur. My mom told me she heard about Dr. Dean Ornish and his approach to heart disease. I googled him and his approach which completely resonated with me. I then talked to a family member that told me they were seeing a naturopathic doctor. I had never heard of these types of physicians. I started researching who they are, what they do as well as patient stories. Yes! This was it. I needed to go find one. From there I made an appointment and did all the lab tests. Wow. She asked me if I had any stress. My labs tests were bad. I had so many food sensitivities, my stress hormones were completely depleted, and I had no good gut bacteria. The bad bacteria were thriving. She felt confident she knew why this happened, how to help me, and the plan made so much sense.

I felt great. I finally knew what my path forward should be. At my next doctor's visit, I told him I didn't want to move forward with the medication. I wanted to try to do this differently. I told him what I learned, the results of these tests, and that I was determined to do the necessary work to heal myself. At first, he was concerned with my approach, but my doctor knew I wasn't the average patient. He supported my decision and told me him he would be there for me in case I got into trouble. I'm so thankful for his approach and his willingness to listen. I was on my own to find my healing journey!

While I worked with my naturopathic doctor, one thing was clear. If this was going to work, the onus was on me. I had to take full responsibility for my health and well-being and start taking care of myself for the rest of my life. I had to do whatever I needed to do to start prioritizing my needs regardless of what anyone else thought. I was in crisis mode, and this was the only way. This wasn't going to be easy since I put myself last for the past thirty years.

One of the greatest needs I had was rest and relaxation. My nervous system was completely depleted given the constant stress and grief. I honestly didn't even know what self-care really was. I thought it was doing an intense work out and eating salad with chicken. Ha! Just like inflammation, I learned self-care is so much more than our physical needs. I learned it's physical, mental, emotional, and spiritual, just to name a few. I now knew what "holistic" meant. Because of my condition, I focused on how our thoughts and emotions can cause inflammation in the body. It's as if the words were speaking to me on the page.

Everything started to finally make sense. My body didn't just start attacking itself. I finally figured out WHY this happened to me! For thirty years I lived with chronic stress and a lot of unprocessed grief. I didn't do anything to take care of myself to get these thoughts and emotions out of my body, mind, and spirit. No one else knew what I was thinking in my mind and all the times I silently cried and worried. I never took care of myself. I never took a break. My mind was always replaying some issue from the past and worrying about something in the future. I was barely in the present. My mind was on overload and as a result, these negative thoughts and emotions traveled down the vagus nerve to my stomach and vice versa. Day by day, negative energy silently transformed into inflammation that settled into the cells of my body, mind, and spirit. It sat there, accumulating and unprocessed, until one day, when Lisa got sick, my body couldn't take anymore just like David's. Chemicals in my food and environment also played a role. All of this wreaked havoc on my insides unbeknownst to me.

While I ultimately figured this all out, I was too far gone, like Lisa, to expect a holistic approach could heal me as quick as I needed it to. It was going to take a LONG time to heal my insides given the damage that had been done. Besides all my other stress at this point, work was crazy with a big company transformation and layoffs going on. The stress was enormous at that time and the pain came back six months into my holistic journey. This time, I had all the old inflammation since the drug never worked along with new inflammation. On top of all that, now my appendix was finally involved. This was spreading just like cancer. My doctor told me I had two choices: go on the drug with a potential risk for PML or have surgery.

All of this threw me for a loop again. I felt to my core that a holistic path was the right way for me and eventually I would be healed. Through one of my breakdowns, that "voice" came back and nudged me for surgery to prevent cancer. Given my father had a history of colon cancer before his lung cancer, this all made sense and I was confident what I must do. I had to get this out ASAP but had learned how to keep it out.

In September 2018, two years after I was diagnosed, I had surgery to remove a foot of my small intestine, an inch of my large intestine and my appendix. After surgery the surgeon came in and surprisingly said, "Catherine, you absolutely made the right decision. There was also a mass that was the size of my fist. I took it out. There was no drug that was ever going to get through that."

Wow. To hear all this after going against what my doctors, surgeon, and what others in my circle thought made me cry. I fought my worries and fears and trusted my intuition. I fought for what I felt was right for me and listened to that "voice" guiding me along the way. Who knew while I was trying to help Lisa with her cancer, God was protecting me from not only Crohn's Disease but from developing cancer? I have no doubt that while God was with Lisa, God was also with me the entire time, guiding me throughout this health crisis. There is no doubt I was being watched over too. I wasn't alone.

It's now been five years since I've been on medication and four years since my surgery. Through a commitment to self-care that serves my body, mind, and spirit, my MRI continues to show no evidence of disease. I am healed and I know it. I'm grateful for everything I've been through and everything I've learned. It's my passion and mission in life to inspire people to take care of themselves no matter what they're going through. I don't want anyone to ever have to learn the hard way like I did to get well, stay well, and be well.

I have learned life is a rollercoaster and it will always be filled with good and bad stress. Some days are filled with grief, regret, fear, anger, and anxiety. Life is also beautiful. Some days are filled with joy, happiness, gratefulness, love, and peace. How do you want to feel? Which life do you want?

Please don't wait to process your grief! If you want to get through your grief with the greatest level of ease, choose to focus on gratefulness for all you've had with your loved one. Be happy they are no longer suffering and for all you have right in front of your face. Choose to spend your time doing things you love. Spend time with people you love. Give your mind space and step into the beauty of nature. Watch your grief fade and your happiness grow.

Put yourself first and practice this simple form of self-care each day. Life is too short to live otherwise. You deserve to be happy and healthy! I hope my story helps you or someone you know get through the pain and inspires you to take care of your body, mind, and spirit. I hope it gets you on the road to health and well-being sooner than you ever thought was possible.

Whenever I'm feeling out of balance, I remind myself how to get back with this quote:

> *If you are depressed, you are living in the past.*
> *If you are anxious, living in the future.*
> *If you are at peace you are living in the moment.*
> —Lao Tzu

I hope this book has shined a light on your grief. Much love to you as you process your grief and continue your journey to health and happiness!

XO
—Catherine

CHAPTER 8

Honoring the Caregiver

In loving memory of Michael Joseph Chille
March 22, 1949 to July 4, 2010

by Patrice McKinley

When I was approached to contribute to this book, I have to say I was hesitant. I wondered what I could contribute. My husband Michael died almost twelve years ago and for the most part, I feel that my personal feelings of grief have passed. To be completely honest, what I felt in the immediate was relieved! Yet how in the world could I tell people I felt this way? How could I be so selfish when he was the one who was so sick and in so much pain? What kind of a horrible person could feel relief when their partner of almost twenty-five years passes away!

My friends and some health professionals told me this of course was normal. After all, Michael's journey with cancer lasted ten years, and anyone taking care of a sick loved one for that long would probably feel this way. Still, I felt guilty, especially because I have two daughters who still grieve the loss their father, who died when they were just teenagers.

I realized though that what I could contribute to this book was my story of what it was like to be the sole caregiver of a spouse going through a long, frightening, painful, and literal fight for his life. So, I agreed to be a part of this healing and inspiring book. Do you know what I have discovered in the process? A new level of healing and assurance for myself! Maybe all the negative feelings that I felt guilty for were in fact normal.

While working on this chapter, I first heard the term "anticipatory grief." When I was going through the caregiving process, I was unable to find the resources that are available today. At that time, I could only find a couple of websites for caregivers, and they weren't helpful to me. Searching the bookstore, I mostly found books about grieving the loss of a loved one who had already passed. For me, learning about anticipatory grief has brought a real sense of—yes, here's that word again—relief. Maybe I wasn't such a selfish person after all.

Now here's the thing: over the years I have shared my honest feelings with many more people than I dared to right after Michael died. I have in fact spoken to mostly other women enduring the absolute overwhelm of their caregiving experience. I have told them that along with the feelings of anxiety, despair, isolation, and depression, it's also perfectly okay to feel anger, impatience, frustration, and maybe even the urge to run away and never look back. That's what I felt. Of course, I never did that, and I was always committed to seeing Michael through whatever was to come. Yet there were many days when I didn't know how I was going to make it. I remember one day I literally just watched my feet on the sidewalk putting one in front of the other. I had no idea how to go on. I spent most of those years in a daze.

The women I spoke to were so grateful to be listened to. I think it gave them a great sense of comfort to be able speak honestly and freely about what they were going through—with someone who had already come out the on other side of it. It can be such a lonely time.

During my caregiving experience, I really had no support system. Both Michael's and my family live out of state, so it was just me taking care of him and our daughters. When he was first diagnosed, the girls were only four and six. I had some wonderful friends that I could say anything to, and they were my lifeline. But fortunately for them, none of them had experienced what I was going through. Some had lost parents but not spouses. They were so loving and caring towards me, and did their best, but they had their jobs and families and lives.

Back to anticipatory grief. The website aplaceformom.com defines anticipatory grief as "the name given to the tumultuous set of feelings and reactions that occur when someone is expecting the death of a loved one." Tumultuous is a good word to describe it. What a roller coaster ride of emotions! There were days of feeling so hopeful, and feeling that things might just be okay, and that Michael would survive this. But then there were the days of watching the person I love writhing in pain. The anguish and powerlessness of that! I felt a total lack of control. Of course, as much as we might try, there is little about death that is within our control.

Here's some of what happened in my family as we were faced with the awful reality that my husband and my children's father had a terminal illness.

Michael was diagnosed with prostate cancer in January of 2000. The day we found out was the day everything in our world changed. Cancer was living in our house now. I felt like I was in a bad movie, and I would keep asking myself, "Is this really happening?"

Of all people, I never thought that Michael would get cancer. He was such a positive, energetic, and spiritual person. He had a holistic counseling practice where, along with regular counseling, he did energy work, hypnosis, and past life regression. This was long before any of these practices became mainstream. He believed strongly in the mind/body connection and body's ability to heal itself with the right mindset and treatments. As a result, when he got the news of his diagnosis, he was not willing to accept surgery as the only way to deal with his cancer.

He asked a lot of questions, spent hours doing research, and talked with people from all over the country to try to decide what he should do. As for me, from the little I knew about prostate cancer, I had heard that it was the most treatable type of cancer. I thought, "Okay, he can have surgery and get his prostate removed, and he won't die from this. We can get through this." But as much as I might choose to do something differently, I understood that ultimately the decision was his to make and I would honor that.

This wasn't easy for me to do though. I just wanted it to be over so we could go on with our lives, but he continued to do his research. Finally, he decided not to have the operation. He felt that he had found enough studies that showed that a person could take the "watchful waiting" approach and have the same outcomes as a man who had their prostate removed so that's what he chose to do.

Michael was very proactive with his treatment. Along with his team of doctors where we live, he regularly saw a radiologist in New York City who used special Color Doppler Ultrasound to make sure that the cancer hadn't spread beyond the prostate. He went to Switzerland on two different occasions for a month at a time to have alternative medical treatments done that weren't available in the US.

For seven years the watchful waiting seemed to be working. Michael was committed to his recovery. He worked with doctors out of state who practiced functional medicine; he did cleanses, took special supplements, and totally changed his diet; he did energy work and hypnotherapy. He found an oncologist in New York that used sound healing therapy. He used a small trampoline that was effective for clearing the lymph system. We got a far infrared sauna. He joined an ashram in Germany and visited a few times. He even went back to the Catholic church and became an active member. He prayed, he visualized, he believed, and he expected to, at the very least, maintain his health and live a fairly normal life.

With every doctor's visit, I would hold my breath, hoping that the results would be good. Anytime I went to any of my own doctors for a checkup of any sort, they would express their concern that he was taking this whole situation too lightly. They told me that this was extremely serious and dangerous, and that he should have surgery. These conversations would undo me. I felt such anxiety and dread. I would come home with these fears and doubts and Michael would try to convince me that he was going to be alright. While I shared many of the same beliefs about spirituality and the power of our minds to create whatever we want, I had a hard time with the belief that he could heal this disease.

Emotionally, I still had questions about how this worked on a physical level. I wasn't at all where Michael was with that belief. I was scared and just wanted him to do something about it. I wanted him to do everything he could, to have surgery and do everything else. I simply had no faith in healing a serious illness through the power of the mind, thoughts, and faith.

My question to myself was always, "Is he doing the right thing? Are we in denial? Are we bargaining?" I guess we were. But he was so sure. I just prayed he was right. I tried to stay as calm and hopeful as I could but inside, I was just holding on.

The first seven years were stressful, but we went on with our lives in as normal a way as we could. We lived. Michael had a thriving horticulture business that he had to tend to, and I oversaw the administrative duties. When he was away in Europe, I was responsible for making sure that everything went smoothly with his employees. In addition, I was keeping up with our school-aged kids and their extracurricular activities. I was so grateful that I didn't have a job outside the home during those years.

I did my best to carve out a life for myself when I could. I became involved in a weekly group coaching program, and I made some great friends from all over the country. Every six months or so we would all meet in San Diego for a four-day intensive training, and these times were so healing for me. In a safe and supportive environment, I was able to share not only what was happening in my present life, but also to think about what I wanted to create for myself in the future. "What did I want?" This gave me such hope. Hope that I could get through what was happening and build a life that I was passionate about.

Being a caregiver can be such a lonely role. My biggest piece of advice to the caregiver would be: any chance you get to do something you love— do it! Whatever it is—gardening, painting, walking on the beach, meditating, dancing, baking, taking a drive with the windows down and singing at the top of your lungs, going out with friends who love and adore you and you can say anything to—find something that is all your own! Since the whole experience can feel like the never-ending treading of water, you must make sure you don't let yourself drown.

I decided to go back to something I loved, and it became my lifeline. I started singing again. I had been a professional singer and had lived in New York City when I was in my early twenties. For reasons that I won't go into here, I moved from New York to Rhode Island and set aside my hopes of singing. Reaching out to friends I had known twenty-five years before in the city, I started working with them to create a solo cabaret show. I had so much fun! I would go to Manhattan for the day and work with my musical director and director, and I felt like myself again! Just for a day I wasn't someone's wife or mother or nurse.

Singing had been such a part of my identity since I was in grade school, and I had just let it go for so long. Now I was doing it again! Whenever I came home from New York, I was renewed. Doing what you love is so important at any time of your life, but I believe it's critical when you are a caregiver. It was not only good for me, but for my whole family.

In the eighth year of his illness, Michael started to have back pain that wouldn't go away. At first, he thought it was just work injury and went to his chiropractor for some adjustments. I was worried! A few weeks later, it was confirmed that the cancer had spread to his bones and his lymph nodes. I remember very well the afternoon we got that phone call from the doctor. I was beside myself. I knew this was the beginning of the end. We just sat on the couch, held each other, and cried. He tried to reassure me once again that he was going to be okay.

Later that day, I simply had to get out of the house to be alone for a little while, so I went to our local Starbucks for a coffee. When I walked in, I saw a good friend of mine with another woman who I knew but not well. I knew I couldn't ignore them, but I was such a wreck, and I didn't want to make a scene. The minute I said hello, I just burst out crying. God works in miraculous ways. I rarely ever see this friend out and about, but there she was in Starbucks, and I sat with them for a long while. The two of them were such a comfort to me just when I really needed it. I didn't know how I was going to get through this. It was already hard. What was this next phase going to be like? The unknown can be such a hard place to be.

From that point on, nothing was the same. There were nights of tears and immense anxiety for both of us, doctor and hospital visits with painful procedures and tests, many trips to the emergency room (why always in the middle of the night?), and two surgeries. He lost about six inches in height because he developed Metastatic Spinal Cord Compression: the cancer had moved into his spine. He suffered with so much physical pain. Most of the time he couldn't climb the stairs to our bedroom by himself, so I would lift his feet one after the other until he reached the top. I could tell you countless stories about the physical caregiving of my husband, but I'll leave it at this: it was exhausting and heartbreaking to watch my vital, energetic husband deteriorate before my eyes.

On our trips to the hospital, most of the ER doctors and the surgeons couldn't believe, from their perspective, that he wasn't taking the cancer more seriously. Some of them were as tactful as they could be when Michael would try to explain his reasoning around his choices, while the other doctors were outraged and extremely blunt. Every time I would hear these conversations, I felt such anxiety and almost embarrassment that my incredibly smart husband was doing this, not just to himself but to our family. But he was an incredibly stubborn man. If he wanted to do something, there was no talking him out of it.

As I am writing this, I'm coming to see that my story is as much about Michael's and my diverging spiritual beliefs and faith as it is about grief and caregiving. After all this time, I am still trying to make sense of it. He believed so strongly in his ability to live through this, but I looked at the facts and the evidence right in front of me. I could see he was not well. When I was alone with the doctors, they told me that he needed to get his affairs in order. I would ask them how long they thought he had. I wanted to know. Of course, no one knows exactly, but I didn't know how much longer I could keep doing this!

Whenever I tried to talk to Michael about the doctors' conclusions, he either discounted them or told me that I wasn't supporting him. One time he told me that it seemed that I just wanted him to die. I told him that I didn't want him to die, but I just wanted all the trauma to be over! I still feel guilty about that. If I had really held the space for his ability to heal, if I had that same level of faith that he did, would that have made a difference?

Now when I read books or articles about how people healed themselves from serious illnesses, I get angry. Why did it work for them and not Michael? He did everything they did. Maybe it was me. Maybe their partners were more supportive of a person's ability to heal. I have no idea.

Michael died on July 4, 2010. Independence Day. That was the day he set himself free. The hospital had called at about 4:30 in the morning and said that we should come now. We surrounded his bed and said our goodbyes, but he was unconscious at that point. As much I tried to prepare myself, watching Michael take his last breath was surreal. I sobbed for about five minutes and from then on, my focus became Julia and Micaela. The girls had known for a few years that their dad had cancer and saw how sick he was, but he really didn't prepare them for the end as he was sure it was not coming. We never had a conversation as a family about the possibility of his death. I had talks with them myself about it, but they never got to say goodbye the way they should have. A few days before his death, he had to be taken away in an ambulance. Before I followed to the hospital, I went into each girl's room separately to tell them that their father was not going to make it. That he was dying. I think that was the hardest thing I have ever had to do in my life. How was I going to help my girls get through this, when I didn't know how I was going to pick up the pieces myself?

The hospital staff gave us all the time we needed in the room with him, and they were so gentle. I have the utmost respect and gratitude for all the nurses who took such good care of us. Talk about caregivers! Thank goodness they, along with our hospice nurses, walked me through how to deal with what was to happen next. I couldn't watch them take his body away. I just couldn't and I didn't want the girls to see that either, so the hospice team took over. When we were leaving, Micaela asked to be alone with her father. It wasn't until a few years later that she told me what she had said.

If I had known that Michael was going to pass that morning, I would have spent the night with him. He had spent nights in the hospital so many times before, and I was so tired that I just wanted to sleep in my own bed. But I didn't know. You just don't know.

Planning the funeral was not fun! I didn't know what I was doing. I had tried to have conversations with Michael about all that a few months before, but he didn't want to talk about it. He had always enjoyed reading the obituaries in the New York Times, so I broached the subject with him, but he deflected. I had to write his obituary, and I know I didn't do him justice.

The day after he passed, after spending hours calling all his friends and breaking the news to them, I went to the funeral home to deal with the "arrangements." I was so blessed to have one of my best friends hold my hand through the process. Caskets, plots, do you need the big room or the small room at the funeral home? Wake or no wake? What day and time? Where will out-of-town guests stay? Is my house clean enough? Who officiates the funeral; who speaks; who will be pallbearers? Where's the reception? Who takes care of the food? Jesus! I understood that this was important for closure. My parents had died years before and I knew what it meant for the family and other people to be able to pay their respects. It can be such a healing time. But at that moment, I felt that I was basically planning a party when I just wanted to be at home with my kids.

We got through it and of course it was lovely. My family and friends were so supportive in every way. People loved Michael. People I had never met told me how he had changed their lives. Parents and friends of our girls came to support them. Old and dear friends of mine that I hadn't seen in years were there. Such true kindness and thoughtfulness and consolation.

Once the funeral was over and family and friends were gone, the reality set in. He wasn't there anymore and never would be. His smile, his creativity, his humor, his gentleness, his love, his stubbornness, his will, and his faith would not be part of our world again. The house was quiet, the energy was totally different. Now it was just the girls and me, and I had to figure out how to move forward.

Everyone who's been through the aftermath of the loss of a loved one knows how much your heart aches trying to let go of all the personal belongings from their full, rich life. You know what the hardest thing for me to let go of? His toothbrush! I could just picture him at the bathroom vanity brushing his teeth. There were days when he was so vital and matter of fact as he got ready for work, and then towards the end, he was in a total trance. Brushing his teeth was such an automatic habit that despite the huge amounts of pain meds he was on; he stood there with his eyes closed, and I just watched him. It was heartbreaking somehow. So, I was able to give up most of his clothes, but that toothbrush stayed in our bathroom for a long time.

Michael had the horticulture business and I had to deal with everything that it involved. His storage facility was filled to the brim with his tools and equipment, and his personal "collections" to put it nicely. He had some valuable antiques mixed in with a lot of junk. I had to figure out what to throw away and what I should try to sell. I had no idea how to clear the space, and it was overwhelming.

A week after he died, a few of his employees met me at the storage unit to start the sorting process. I had rented a dumpster, and they had started throwing stuff out before I arrived. When I got there, I noticed a goldfinch sitting on the windowsill of the unit with its wings outstretched. I wasn't sure if it was dead or just stunned. I have seen stunned birds before, but never one with outstretched wings. How did this bird get in? It had been days since I had been there and no one else had access. The guys hadn't gotten there long before me, and I asked Michael's employee Jonathan if he knew where the bird had come from. He said it was on the window when he arrived. Jonathan had been working for Michael for nine years, starting when he was fourteen years old, and Michael had become like a father figure to him. Jon moved the bird outside onto some grass, and I just stood there staring at it for a while. Eventually I had to get home, so I left the bird where it was. I asked Jon later if he had done anything with it. He said it wasn't there anymore, and he assumed it had flown away.

Michael had been a huge bird lover his whole life. Before I met him, he bred canaries. He had bird feeders everywhere outside our house. We even had a bird clock in our kitchen that made a different bird call every hour. It was a big conversation piece among visitors. Jon and I agreed that somehow this goldfinch must have been a sign.

A few months later I was clearing out my garage and basement, both also stacked to the ceiling with Michael's things. How do you know what to throw away? I had to go through everything so carefully because I didn't know what would be in some way valuable. As I was going through one of the many boxes of his memories, I came upon a plastic model of a goldfinch with its wings outstretched! It looked just like the one at the storage unit! My brother-in-law was there helping me with some household repairs and when I showed him, he said that Michael had made the bird when he was a kid. He had made models of a cardinal and a blue jay as well, but the only one I found was the goldfinch. Now that bird has a very special place in our living room and every time we see a real goldfinch anywhere, we feel Michael must be near.

While I was writing this chapter, Jonathan got married. I know Michael would have been so happy for him. Jon's new wife, who had never known Michael but knew how much Jon loved him, gave him a beautiful set of cufflinks with golden birds on them. How beautiful is that! It was so touching to me. I think she's a keeper!

My caregiver job didn't end when Michael's life did. I continued to take care of everything: Selling the house, the sadness the girl's experienced with the selling of the house, getting rid of all the stuff, repairs, finances, death certificates, selling the business, and the five dumpsters worth of a "life" we had to let go of. But with all that came the support of my brother, sister, my dearest friends, and even people I really didn't know. They all touched me so deeply and I will never forget. There is so much goodness in people and I am forever grateful for all that was shown to me. The healing that I was graced with from all these acts of kindness was immeasurable.

My grief, my sadness continued as I watched my daughters grieve. Michael had been such a great dad and I really miss my children's father. I miss being able to talk to him about the girls and what they are going through. No one will love them like I love them except Michael.

Through the twelve years he's been gone, Julia and Micaela have been through a lot. It hasn't been easy for either one of them. They both still have recurring dreams about him. The gist of them is that he's back and they are so happy to see him, but they know he's probably going to leave again. My heart breaks for them and there is nothing I can say to make it better. That's a tough place to be as a mother. But despite it all, they are finding their way and making lives for themselves.

I am too. I became certified as a coach in yet another program that I absolutely love, and I have been helping so many people become aware of their own inner power to really live their purpose. It's incredibly rewarding and inspiring to see someone step out of a box of limitation and into a life beyond their imagination.

Richard Bach said that "we teach best what we most need to learn" and I am no exception. I know I was living in a box. Even before Michael's diagnosis, I had my own issues of anxiety and depression. I was a recovering alcoholic of many years, but I was also an active food addict. While Michael was sick, my food addiction was out of control. About three years after he died, I was able to take charge of my health not just for myself, but for my girls' sake, and I lost seventy-five pounds.

I have to say writing my story for this book about grief hasn't been easy. It has brought up a lot of feelings and memories that are hard to revisit. But it also made me realize how far I've come. I have created a life for myself. My beautiful daughters are making their way in the world, and I am so proud of who they've become. I have a career that I love, I have siblings and friends who mean the world to me, I live in a healthy body, and I am still singing.

Michael and I disagreed about the details of how he should care for his illness, but my spirituality and how I pass so much of that on to others now in my work is strong and he was indeed a building block for that. The shame, or at least the confusion I carried around in different degrees about my feeling of relief when he passed is long gone. There is no gold watch given to the caregiver, especially if the result is not ideal, but there are also no rules and no mistakes. Seek out all the ways you can to take care of yourself and love yourself so that you will have the energy and patience you need to take care of your loved one. Maybe most of all, try not to judge any of your feelings as you are living this sad yet somehow privileged experience and know with the utmost certainly—you are not alone, you will get through this, and you will come out the other side. I have.

CHAPTER 9

Diane is Dancing in Heaven!

*In loving memory of my big sisters Diane and Beverly
thank you for continuing to watch over us*

by Carrie Beers

My morning of September 9, 2020 started like every other morning until my phone rang at 6:30 a.m. Fear immediately took over when I saw it was my little sister. My heart sank. I gripped the phone tightly preparing myself. I said "Hello," and there was a pause. I could feel her sorrow through the phone. She was calling to let me know our sister Diane had slipped into a coma and most likely would not live through the day. No one had been able to see Diane since she was rushed to the hospital a few days prior. Now, her husband and daughters were on their way to the hospital to be by her side to say goodbye. I felt anger at COVID circumstances preventing me from racing to the hospital to be by her side.

Knowing our only connection to our big sister right now was sisterhood, my younger sister and I stayed on the phone silently, not wanting to break the connection. During our silence on the phone, I wondered, *Did Diane know no one was there? Did she understand why we could not be with her? Would it have made a difference if she had visitors? Could she have fought her way back again if she heard our voices or felt our touch?* I had not even talked to her; she had been too weak to hold her phone. DAMN COVID!

My little sister and I finally said goodbye, breaking our connection. I just sat shaking, tears falling uncontrollably. I needed to distract myself. I tried to get up to eat but could not. I knew I should be calling people but could not. I could not move or function. I gave in to my tears and the heart wrenching sorrow seeping into every cell of my body.

I just sat waiting, longing to be with her. I hate waiting! Although she had been dying for years, I was stunned that today would probably be the day my sister Diane would join my sister Beverly, Mom, and Dad in heaven. I thought I was prepared for this day. I felt as though I had been grieving for her since her health began failing. I was surprised at how raw I felt. I guess it does not matter whether you get the call that a loved one died suddenly or that their battle was finally over. It is not possible to "be emotionally prepared" for the dreaded moment you learn someone you love died.

My mind began racing with memories. It felt like I was watching a movie reel in fast forward. They were fast, blurry and would stop randomly.

When it stopped, I saw myself sitting in my little sister's living room on the day Diane told us she learned her kidneys were beginning to fail, a result of a chronic illness she had been battling since she was about nineteen years old. Standing in front of us, she firmly told us she did not and would not give either of us permission to be a kidney donor for her. We tried to argue with her, but her certainty made us stop arguing. We could see the conviction in her decision. She was rejecting our kidneys. That conversation was so many years ago.

Not long after that meeting, Diane began living her health nightmare. It was tough watching her body fail. I was scared every time she developed new health challenges. It was upsetting standing by watching her spirit dim a bit every time her illness took away her ability to do something she had done a thousand times before.

Diane and I began to spend more time together. I knew how important it was for her to have dreams to fight her illness, so I started asking her questions and encouraging her to tell me about her dreams. No surprise, all her dreams focused on being with her family.

She wanted to watch all her girls get married. She was able to stand proudly by beaming as two of her daughters said, "I do."

She wanted to meet, play, and create things with her grandchildren. She proudly welcomed four grandchildren into the family and loved spending time playing and making homemade ornaments with them each Christmas.

She wanted to grow old with her husband. Was that still a possibility? It did not seem likely.

I believe having dreams saved and served her through the years. There were countless times we were told to prepare for the worst, then watched in amazement as Diane fought her way back, defying the odds to be with her husband, her girls, her grandchildren, and her family.

Over time we would affectionately say she was like the Energizer Bunny. She just kept going. I attributed her will to her awareness and emotional connection to her dreams. I recall one health scare that her dreams helped her fight her way back to us.

I received a call from her husband one morning. Diane was back in the hospital. She was weak from not being able to eat due to complications associated with her illnesses. He had to get to the office and felt horrible leaving her. I cancelled all my clients and rushed to go be with her.

When I arrived at her room a nurse was trying unsuccessfully to get her to take a sip of a protein drink. Through her half coherent state Diane was shaking her head slowly no. She even found the strength to clamp her lips closed. The nurse turned and looked at me. I understood. There were only two options: open her mouth and take a few sips of the protein drink, or she faced them inserting a feeding tube. No way would she want a feeding tube. I asked the nurse if I could sit with her for a bit and try. She gladly handed me the drink.

Wiping away my tears, I put my fear aside, pulled up a chair, and began talking quietly to Diane about her daughters, husband, her first grandchild (her other three grandchildren were not with us yet), and all she loved about her life. Her face was turned towards me, her eyes glazed so I could not tell if she heard me. Every few minutes I would lightly tap the straw to her lips, begging her to take a sip. She just kept them tightly shut looking at me, pleading for me to stop. I lost track of how long this went on. I do remember at one point being so agitated with her I wanted to scream. Instead, I leaned down close to her ear, this time my lips tight, teeth clenched and stated, "Not taking a sip isn't an option."

I reminded her she was in the hospital and if she continued to fight taking a sip on her own, they would insert a feeding tube down her throat. Whatever her plan was, it was not realistic based on where she was. I became obsessed with getting her to take a damn sip. Every few minutes I tapped the straw to her dry lips, willing her to sip. Finally, she took a sip, then another. I remember feeling myself relax and smile when she had consumed half of the drink. Quickly my smile faded when she opened her eyes, looked at me with such distaste, and simply turned away, dismissing me.

She slept while I sat mortified at her reaction. Wondering why. Did she understand the alternative? I began questioning my motive. Was I selfish in forcing her to drink? Did I do the right thing? I hated feeling this emotional rollercoaster when a decision had to be made and she had me questioning if I made the wrong one. Soon I felt pissed at her. Pissed she wanted to give up. Pissed that sometimes as her caregiver we had to make decisions she might not like. Pissed that I was here. My anger simmered just below the surface for the rest of the day.

Over the next few weeks, she was able to find the will to fight back and leave the hospital. I am glad her dreams to be with her family outweighed any other thought she might have had during her hospital stay.

I did not expect, nor will I forget, the fallout we had after she left the hospital regarding my stance at her bedside making her take a sip of the drink.

I did not realize how angry she was until months later. I was visiting and she asked if I wanted something to drink. As I got up to get one, she lashed out and said, "I'm perfectly capable of getting you a drink." It took her so much effort and time to get up and moving. It was hard to watch. I learned to be patient. I knew it was important for her to maintain her independence. She stopped after taking one or two steps. Walking was becoming just too much for her fragile body. I felt her anger when suddenly she turned and told me how angry she was at me for making her drink the protein drink in the hospital.

Stunned I simply asked, "Why?"

She responded, "You shouldn't have forced me to drink, you should have let me go." She added, "It's not up to you whether I live or die, you're not God."

Those words will forever live in my memory. We got into an argument;

no scratch that, we got into a screaming match. We yelled back and forth, both of us adamant about our position. This type of arguing became our norm as her illness progressed. Neither of us noticed when our tears of anger turned to tears of joy, clinging to each other thankful she was still alive.

When I left her, I started shaking on the way to my car. I managed to get the key in the ignition to start the car but then froze and wondered, was she right, did I overstep in the hospital? Was my goal of getting her to drink more for me than her? Did my caring for her become about what I wanted versus what she needed or wanted? I absolutely did not want to lose my sister, but was it my place to force her to do things? Have I been disregarding her desire for my own desire? When or how do you know? When do you let go? These questions troubled me all the way home.

It took hours of journaling and thinking time to sort my feelings out. During this process I realized that even my prayers for her seemed more about what I wanted and not what she wanted. I forced myself to rethink what was best for her versus what I wanted for her. This included modifying my prayers for her. Immediately my prayers became about honoring what Diane desired, not what I desired. When faced with a decision, I reminded myself to put her needs first.

Sitting remembering that argument, how I wished today she were yelling at me from her hospital bed now. Not in a coma, fighting for her life. I just wanted to hold her hand, tell her how much I loved her, to hug and kiss my big sister goodbye. I had zero confidence there would be another miracle remembering seeing her deteriorated condition upon my arrival back to Rhode Island to visit her in July. Both her body and her will deteriorated so fast I could feel she lost her will to live. I began to pray. I prayed that she was without pain and at peace. I prayed she found peace and comfort. I asked God to calm her soul. I prayed Beverly, Dad, and Mom were with her.

I recall that day in July when I first saw Diane, the shock of seeing how rapidly her condition had changed in the brief time I was gone. Her energy had changed, and I knew her will had changed. In that moment, I knew I had to end my business road trip and return home quickly. I wanted to spend time with my sister before it was too late.

I struggled with the drastic change in her health upon my return. She had zero strength to sit up, she struggled to keep her eyes open, even speaking had become challenging. I expected changes in her health. I did not expect the severity of the changes. It was scary. How did she become a shell of my sister, clinging to life? I could not even imagine how isolated and lonely she must have felt for the last several months in and out of healthcare facilities with no loved ones allowed to be by her side due to COVID protocols. No wonder she was ready to give up.

I dreaded leaving again, but I had no choice but to get my things. I did not know when I would resume traveling.

I kept thinking the same thing over and over. What happened to my sister I said goodbye to just six months earlier? My sister who was smiling and laughing, happier than she has been in years. My sister who encouraged me to start living my life again. My sister who made me promise to send pictures and call her often so she could hear of my adventures and how my business was growing. My sister who had fought for years to live. My sister who hugged and kissed me goodbye admitting she was scared. Then told me how proud she was of me for having the courage to go across the country on my own. Reminding me I had an angel with me, our sister Beverly. Yes, Diane's body had been failing before I left, but this was different. Now her light was dimming.

The day I left, I prayed to God to honor what she desired, to release her from her pain, even if it meant I would not make it home in time. My prayer became simple: "If it was her desire to stop fighting, please honor her wishes. If her desire is to fight to live another day, please honor her wishes." It was between Diane and God now.

As I sat on my couch remembering that awful day, I felt deflated with no hope. I found myself wanting to find positive memories of Diane. I grabbed my phone and began scrolling through photos hoping to find something positive. Soon I was staring at a picture of Diane and her two daughters. Immediately I felt all the joy from that day. It was earlier this year, January 26, 2020, the day my big sister Diane turned sixty. Her celebration was small, just the way she wanted it. Diane wanted to be with the people she loved most. The people who stuck with her through her nightmare.

The morning of her birthday I awoke excited for Diane. I could not wait to see her. My phone rang and my heart stopped, praying, no not today. It was her husband. Diane's day did not start off on a positive note—she had fallen. He thought she should go to the emergency room, but she was resisting. She did not want her party cancelled. We got her to compromise when we indicated the decision to cancel the party could wait until they met with the doctor in the emergency room. I was not sure which way it would go.

For hours I waited as did the rest of the family, wondering if her party would be canceled. She made her husband call us from the emergency room and through her pain, bruises, and cuts, she insisted she would be okay and again begged us not to cancel the party yet. We gladly waited—no one wanted to cancel. It was getting closer to the time her party was to start when, finally, she received decent news. Relieved nothing was broken, the doctors saw no reason she could not attend her celebration although they hoped she would not. She decided to go ahead with the party.

Diane arrived late. She rolled into the room wearing her signature smile, amidst purple bruises, raw cuts still swollen, and her pain. She looked radiant. There seemed to be a collective exhale when everyone saw her smiling. Her smile had a powerful effect on people. Everyone relaxed ready to celebrate Diane.

Her four grandchildren ran up to her yelling, "Happy Birthday, Mimi Di," and hugged her. They did not see her injuries, just her. Her tender body hurt from their hugs, but nothing was going to stop her from trying to embrace all of them at once. She held them tightly, laughing and smiling, welcoming their kisses, hugs, laughter, and endless chatter. Her birthday may have started off rough but during her celebration I could see her temporarily letting go of the pain. She embraced being alive and made sure she spent time with each person. As she moved around the room, we all witnessed her resilience, courage, and desire to live. Diane's love for everyone showed as we celebrated her sixtieth birthday. I sat back and basked in the joy and love surrounding her. I got a glimpse of the vibrant, energetic, and life of the party sister she once was.

She glowed from the love surrounding her. I watched her talking to our little sister, remembering the childhood mischief and fun all of us got into throughout the years. We drove our parents crazy and absolutely tested their patience. I could not have asked for better sisters. Even with all the challenges our relationships had over the years, we remained close. I knew I could count on each one of my sisters to drop everything without hesitation to be there for me. As I would for them. No one protects you better than your sisters. We always found a way to cheer each other on when life tried to keep one of us down, and we were the first to celebrate the tiniest milestone. Tears came to my eyes sitting there remembering, thinking, *I am not ready to lose another sister.*

Diane's birthday party was my last family function for a while, making the day even more bittersweet. I was ecstatic Diane was enjoying herself. As I watched her saying goodbye to everyone, my eyes were drawn to her discolored, swollen cheek, the various cuts on her face and body, her eyes beginning to show pain and tiredness. How could I leave now? Guilt and fear were creeping back into my thoughts. I did not know what to do. Does the rest of the family think I am being selfish? Are they angry with me for leaving? Did they even know why I was going through with my trip? My guilt about leaving extended to her husband and other family members left to care for her. It took all of us. I was one of her caregivers, drivers, companions, and most importantly her sister. Wasn't it my obligation to stay and help? I needed to talk to Diane again.

It was not to be an easy conversation. I had just returned from a trial trip from August to November 2019 that Diane made me promise to take. I had been delaying the start of my dream trip I had planned to start in 2018 that would have me away from home for about two years. Since I was twenty years old, I wanted to travel around the US, stopping where I wanted to explore all the beauty, great landmarks, and get to know the people in each state. I even built my business in a way that would allow me to be mobile and work anywhere while fulfilling my dream. I kept finding reasons to delay my departure to help care and spend time with Diane. How could I leave? She needed so much support it took all of us chipping in to help her husband.

In the summer of 2019, Diane called me out, not wanting me to delay my trip any longer. She was on to me. It had been over a year since I completed the final preparations to embark on my dream trip. I sold everything and rented rooms in a friend's home for what should have only been for a few months but turned into over a year. Diane had setbacks during this time and that was how I started delaying. I always felt the timing was off.

When I agreed to the trial trip, I designed it so I remained on the East Coast. I wanted to see how I felt being away from Diane. I wanted reassurance her health was stable.

The business side of the trip went amazing. Suddenly looking towards 2020, I was optimistic about having a wonderful year. Being able to focus on the business without disruption made me realize how I longed to get into full swing with my business again. As excited as I was to escape and be able to focus on my life and business, I also felt guilty about not being home.

The personal pull to be back home was tough. My emotions kept swinging this way and that way. I loved finally living my dream. I was in my element focused on my business and spending time with friends I knew along the way. I loved the days when I felt myself expanding and basking in the freedom. I loathed the days that felt heavy from the weight of my guilt for feeling happy. It was frustrating and often affected my focus and productivity. Guilt became my travel partner during the long drives between destinations.

It was frustrating living with guilt all the time, so I adopted a practice of questioning any guilt or negative emotions that would surface. When I had an emotion or feeling that was counterproductive to how I wanted to be while traveling, I would pause and ask, "Why are you really feeling this emotion? Is it coming from your heart or from your head?" Then I would listen to my body and think myself through to the answer. Next, I would ask, "Does this emotion serve any part of your life today?" If I got a yes, I would repeat the process again to see if it was my truth. Very rarely was it my truth. When the answer was no, I released the emotion and replaced it with a positive emotion by filling in the blank of this statement: "I AM now feeling..." My next step was to write a new "I AM" statement on a sticky note and post it where I could see it. I posted the positive statements to keep my spirits up and to change my thinking. Let me tell you there were a bunch of sticky notes posted.

The exercise and notes really helped me stay focused and in the right headspace when I needed to conduct business. I began to feel less guilt about wanting to live my life as my sister fought for hers. I reviewed these sticky notes daily and before I would call to talk to Diane. I wanted to present a cheerful outlook with her. She did not need to worry about me.

When my trial trip ended, I drove north back to Rhode Island subdued with so much uncertainty in my life. I arrived home for the holidays and Diane's sixtieth birthday celebration. It was time to assess things and decide when I would go back out on the road. The times I spoke to Diane from the road, she seemed to be the same, but I needed to see for myself how she was. When I arrived home, I had to wait until I quarantined before I could see either of my sisters. It was so frustrating.

It felt great when I finally visited Diane. I sighed with relief seeing that she was holding steady and seemed a bit better. It was nice sharing my adventures with her in person. She loved hearing my stories. It was like old times when we talked about the business connections and opportunities I was considering. She offered great advice and pointed out areas of concern. Sitting talking reminded me of all the times we offered each other advice about our careers, dealing with some conflict, or simply celebrating one of our successes.

Eventually we addressed the elephant in the room. When should I leave again? She did not want to hear any excuses or plans to delay staying, she wanted me to leave right after her birthday. I said, "I was not ready to decide. Let's enjoy being together and getting ready for the holidays and your birthday."

She was not going to wait. She sat up straighter, leaned towards me, determined for me to really hear and feel what she had to say, "Stop making excuses and start living your life." What she said next still haunts me: "I feel like you are waiting for me to die, and I cannot handle that." Those words went right to my heart, my core, as chills ran up my arms. In that moment it hit me. She was feeling just as guilty about me staying as I did about me leaving. How insensitive of me for not thinking about how my decision affected her. Followed by the thought she might be right. Was I waiting for her to die?

You bet I was hesitant. I was terrified to leave her, to open myself up to getting another one of those heart wrenching calls. I know too well the horror of being over 2500 miles away and receiving "the call" that a loved one passed away. The hardest two calls I ever received announced the unexpected death of my sister Beverly and a plea urging me to get home before my father passed away. I did not make it in time to say goodbye to Dad. I was in the Denver airport when I called home to check on him and learned I was too late.

Even remembering these calls now sends chills up my spine. I knew too well the feeling of shock, isolation, and fear. Scrambling to get flights, the nightmare of packing, trying to hold back tears as I stood in line waiting to board each plane or frustrated with delays. Seeing the face of the family member waiting at the airport. Clinging to them, letting go of all the tears I did not dare shed during my journey home. I did not want to share my fears with her as she sat waiting for my response. She did not need to know I still get chills whenever a family member calls me at an odd time. No one knew, until I wrote this now.

I felt out of excuses. I agreed and promised to leave after her birthday party. It was the hardest promise I have made to date.

I kept my promise and at 4:00 a.m. on January 29, 2020, with a heavy heart and mixed emotions, I set out to continue my road trip. As I crossed the border into Connecticut, I wanted to turn around, but her words haunted me and kept my foot on the pedal heading south away from her.

I was a little surprised at the conflicting emotions I experienced as the distance between me and her grew greater. I expected to feel torn and worried about leaving, wondering what might happen while I was gone. I did feel that. What I did not expect was how quickly my excitement grew even though I left her so soon after her fall. Excitement about truly starting my dream, not just testing being away this time. I could not wait to grow my business in a new direction.

My business did well during the years of my sister's illness, but I did not have the desire to grow it. It was not anything anyone asked me to do. I just felt a need to be available for her and honestly, I no longer possessed the drive to build my business. My dream faded to the background of my life as I was worried about my sister. Driving away again, I felt a bit relaxed that I was escaping being a caregiver. Although leaving gave me the freedom to pursue my dreams again, it came with so much guilt.

My first stop was to spend time with a good friend in New Jersey. I was looking forward to girl time and relaxing. On my second night there I received a call from Diane's husband to let me know she had a setback but would be okay. He said Diane encouraged me to continue my trip.

I landed in North Carolina in late February. The plan was to be there for a few months before heading west. On my second day I got word that Diane was back in the hospital, but she was out in a couple of days. A week later, she went into the hospital and this time she had to get rehab to build her strength up, so she left the hospital and went to a rehabilitation facility. By now my emotions where like a yo-yo.

I was living the nightmare I feared. Going home was not that easy. I had commitments on the road, and I could not stay with either of my sisters. My options seemed limited, but I knew staying away was not possible. I had to get home. I began working on my return plan. As I was working out the details to get back home, the pandemic became a reality, and the world was in turmoil.

Too quickly things began to get scary with COVID. The news that New York and New Jersey were closing their states with stay-at-home orders made travel challenging. Soon Interstate 95 rest areas shut down and all non-essential travel had been halted, followed by a domino effect for all travel options. Rhode Island followed suite and implemented a stay-at-home order on March 28, 2020. States banned non-residents entering and quarantines were implemented for residents traveling home. Air travel and public transportation stopped. I watched all this unfold while stuck724 miles away from my sister, my home, my loved ones. To say I was terrified is an understatement. The dominoes just kept falling around me.

It was horrible thinking how isolated my sister was at home. She sat in a rehabilitation facility trying to get her strength back, trying to fight to live, with no one allowed to visit. Every time I spoke to her husband and daughters, I felt their sorrow and frustration from being kept away from her. All I wanted to do was hug them, be with them.

At one point her husband resorted to standing outside her window so they could at least see one another. Eventually even that little connection was no longer an option. Diane's nightmare would continue with her back and forth between the hospital and rehabilitation facilities until

July 2020. During this entire time never seeing loved ones, feeling her husband's touch or his kiss. Diane may not have contracted COVID, but all the mandates preventing her from seeing her loved ones contributed to her quality of life and her will to fight.

While Diane was fighting to recover, I sat in a room isolated from my family, desperate to get home. I felt trapped. I would take drives and walks, but nothing helped. How I longed for a conversation with her. I tried to keep my promise to call and send her photos, but she struggled to hold her phone so talking became impossible. The healthcare workers scheduled time for her to talk with her husband and daughters and I am thankful they did. There was no way they had time for all of us to talk to her. I felt yet another barrier thrown in my way preventing me from communicating with Diane.

One rainy afternoon I was feeling trapped, frustrated, hurt, sad, and pissed. I was pissed at myself for leaving Rhode Island. I was pissed at the pandemic. I was pissed at Diane for not fighting. I was just pissed! My blood pressure was rising while my heart was racing. I could feel a panic attack coming on. At least I thought it was a panic attack. I had to do something fast. I found one of my guided meditations to help me settle my heartbeat and calm my mind. Thankfully, it worked.

Jumping into action would help so I began looking for a place to live back home. Finding a place proved challenging. Overnight the housing market became inflated followed by limited to no inventory. I have never seen every potential type of living quarters available affected so quickly. Call after call I received the same response: too late, already gone. I felt pressure to find something. On July 4, I felt a nudge to go back and look at rental options. It did not make sense I had looked earlier, but I learned long ago to listen to these nudges, my intuition. A new listing had just been posted; I reached out immediately and got a response. I put the place on hold to view it when I could return to Rhode Island. The owner was willing to wait. Finally, I was able to head back into Rhode Island in late July. I would get to see how Diane was doing and secure a place to live. The place on hold was available September 1, 2020. I grabbed it. I was relieved. I had a place to come home to even if it was only a short-term rental from September to May. It was time to rush back to North Carolina and get back to Rhode Island.

Driving away and leaving was even harder this time, knowing Diane was failing daily. There was a sense of urgency to get back. I did not feel comfortable traveling. The pandemic still wreaked havoc everywhere. It was eerie traveling down a major interstate with few cars and restrooms empty. I had to be extremely careful traveling. I could not get COVID and be stuck in North Carolina. I felt like there was a stopwatch tracking every second it took me to get back to Rhode Island. Thankfully, I had a friend who opened her home to me in Rhode Island until my rental was ready in September. I returned to Rhode Island on August 21, 2020.

Something brought me back to sitting on my couch, waiting. I looked at the clock and noticed it was noon. On cue my stomach rumbled to feed it. It had been hours since I talked to my little sister. As each hour passed, I dared to feel a bit of hope. Was I wrong? Would Diane again beat the odds and return to us? Then I came back to reality remember the lifeless look of her eyes, her inability to talk or sit up when I last saw her ten days before. Thinking of that last visit breaks my heart while it also brings a smile to my face, especially our conversation the day after the visit.

Diane wanted both of her sisters over to celebrate our August birthdays. I was excited that Diane was coherent and wanting time with us. We got her favorite food and headed to her home. Her husband met us at the door, sad. As we approached, we stopped talking and waited. Diane woke up excited and spent extra time on her care to be ready for us. Unfortunately, the littlest excursion left her exhausted. She had fallen asleep before we arrived, and he could not wake her. We tried too; she would open her eyes, say a few words, and then drift off. We stayed, hoping she would wake up, but she did not. Heavy hearted, we left.

The next day I spoke to Diane. She expressed how excited she was that she woke up and spent time visiting with us. I did not want to hurt her. I agreed it was great spending time visiting and talking. When I hung up, I thought she must have heard us even though she was sleeping deeply. I thought it best if we let her think she was awake during our visit. Her husband and my little sister happily agreed. Sitting here I am so glad we let her believe she spent another sister birthday with us.

I glanced at my watch; it was a few minutes before 3:00 p.m. I closed my eyes for a minute, overwhelmed. Suddenly I had a vision of my sister

Diane with her legs intact, wearing her signature smile, her body healthy, vibrant, floating up to heaven. In a flash I saw Diane dancing in heaven with our sister Beverly. They were twirling and giggling, laughing, and crying as they danced creating a light with every dance move. The light became so bright, eventually I could no longer see them. As their vision became blurred and then gone from my sight, a new yet familiar feeling was seeping into my bones, my cells, my being, thesame feeling I felt when my sister Beverly's body physically left this earth, but her spirit remained close to all her sisters.

Instantly I was reminded that the bond of sisterhood would always tether us together, uniting us in a unique way. My big sisters will continue to protect me and my little sister as we continue to walk this earth. We will feel them encouraging us to soar higher, live authentically, and love wholeheartedly.

My mom once told me, "You must be willing to hurt 100 percent if you want to love 100 percent." My sisters are telling us, "Itis okay to hurt 100 percent for now." My little sister and I now had two guardian sister angels. In time, they would remind me to live and love again 100 percent.

My phone ringing at 3:15 p.m. brought me back to reality. I reached for the phone, my hands shaking. I answered it with my heart in my throat, tears running down my face. I heard my little sister's voice quiver with her own tears, and I knew Diane lost her fight. Heaven received a new angel today. A dancing one!

We both began hurting 100 percent. We did not know what to do next; we just sat on the phone crying. Crying the tears you only cry when you lose a sister, feeling the shift in how our hearts would beat a little differently going forward. I know this wrenching feeling of a vice grip closing over your heart in a certain way from the call that first introduced me to this horrific grieving, the call I received when my oldest sister, Beverly, passed away. I am devastated that both my big sisters are gone, yet strangely happy they are together again.

Hanging up the phone, I felt lost; I did not know what to do. Usually, we would all gather to mourn and remember our loved one. COVID was preventing us from being able to gather. There would be no sharing a meal, crying in between bites. No stories would be told, honoring Diane's life.

There would be no big celebration of her life. I felt Diane was robbed of the celebration she deserved. Damn COVID!

Instead, I called people to let them know she was gone. I appreciated their kind words, but it felt so clinical and task oriented. The phone just did not cut it. The whole thing did not feel right. I felt disconnected and lost. I would feel this way for a long time.

I felt trapped and had to get out. I grabbed my keys and went for a drive. Not the best idea. I had trouble seeing through my tears. I was living by the ocean, so I just pulled over, parked, and stared at the water focused on the horizon.

The ocean was always my safe place, but not today. I felt isolated with my grief. I felt cheated. I had rushed back to Rhode Island to be with her and only saw her twice and now she was gone. My head knew that she was in a better place, at peace, and without pain. I was glad that Diane's suffering was finally over. I knew she was whole again and smiling. But I kept wishing I could have had more time with her. I wish I could have said goodbye to her.

Once again, I felt like a movie reel was running through my mind, but this time it was not good memories. They were moments I wished I could change. Times when Diane called and wanted me to come over and watch a movie, eat a meal, or just visit. I went most of the time, but today I could only remember the times I did not go.

It did not matter if I had plans, work, or something else to do, I was consumed with regret for not going. I could hear her disappointment over the phone when I said I could not come over. I saw her sitting all alone longing for a visitor. Her husband did what he could, but he had work and had things to do.

I sat trying to justify my actions. Thinking I only did not go when I had client meetings, training, or other business stuff needing my attention. But that is not the truth. Sometimes I simply needed a break from her. It began to hurt too much watching her illness progress. Seeing her lose more independence. Sometimes I just needed time for me.

Now I wished I had gone every time. It would have given me more time with her. My logical mind knows that it was okay to put myself first sometimes, but today there was no logic, just hurt, guilt, and anger. Diane was primarily house-bound for years and only family went to visit. My anger shifted direction to all the friends who faded away as Diane's health failed. She was always there for friends; where were they when she needed friendship and companions? We would talk about it every now and then. She was so sad about everyone disappearing over the years. Even though she knew they were just living their lives, it still hurt her. I was just mad at the world right then.

My thoughts turned towards all the times I would take her to appointments, we would go for a meal, or go shopping. Taking her out was challenging. She got out so infrequently she always had a list of all she wanted to do. Usually it was fine, but sometimes it was grueling. She wanted to keep her independence, I got that. But there was no such thing as a quick errand. Especially when she had to use a walker and eventually a wheelchair. I recall one of the worse days we were out, when I got mad and did not hide it from her.

It was during the Christmas season, and we had been shopping for hours. I was tired and hungry. Diane insisted on using her walker, not her wheelchair. I got it, she wanted to walk as much as possible, but the weather was cold, the crowds large, and the people unfriendly. We were at our fourth store to pick up her husband's gift. Of course, there were delays finding and paying for the gift. Eventually we got back to the car. I got Diane, her walker, and packages in, and as I went to start the car, and heard Diane mumble, "I think I forgot my debit card in the store." I reacted and snapped, not good.

She started crying as she looked through her purse for her card. She could not find it. She opened the door ready to go back in. I said I would quickly run in. She took offense at me stopping her, as at this point, she was hangry and tired too. She said, "Just leave me, I'll walk home." Yelling ensued as did tears from both of us. I ran into the store and the card was not there. I got back to the car, and she was holding it. It was in her pocket. I did not say a word. We originally planned to grab a bite to eat, but both of us were so angry she asked me to take her home. I did.

After dropping her off, my level of angst for the way I reacted was off the charts. I could not believe I lost my patience with her. I understood her need to remain as independent as possible. Hell, I would want my independence too. But I am human and sometimes I wanted the easy way, not the right way to get things done with her. My logical brain could not let this go today and I cried for not being patient.

I carried that day around for about six months when I decided to do something about it. I decided to use my daily journaling practice to write about all the good times we spent together and all the wonderful trips out we had. It was important that I kept it real and documented all my emotions, good and bad, during this journal exercise. Once I wrote a journal entry, I would reread it, pause wherever I mentioned an emotion and ask questions about the emotion. I would ask "Why?" followed by "Does emotion any longer serve me, or should I let it go?" I chose to let go of all the negative emotions and only hold on to the positive moments of the memory.

Remembering this exercise, I decided to grab my phone and find a positive outing to write about. I came across a series of photos Diane asked me to take. The event was one of the darkest parts of Diane's journey. But this part of that dark time had some beautiful moments. It still hurts to think about parts of it, but the pure joy in this picture of what Diane experienced outweighs everything else. It was just what I needed.

I went back to a time when it had been two years since she walked because her body struggled to heal her foot. She was depressed and devastated that she may lose her leg. One day she called me and asked if I would come over and help change her thinking. She wanted the right mindset for either outcome. I laugh when I think of the way she asked. When she called, she simply said, "Can you help me think more like you?" I jumped at the chance to help her. We spent time developing a plan, actions she could take, and she set goals. She developed a mantra of saying, "This is all part of my journey to reach my goals."

Unfortunately, she lost one of her legs from the knee down. She would eventually lose the other leg from the knee down for the same reason.

The photo I landed on was just after the final fitting of her first prosthetic leg. We had been going to the orthotics and prosthetic facility for weeks. It was a lengthy process; measuring, fitting, and getting everything perfect so Diane would not injure herself. This day Diane would take a huge step towards achieving the goals she set. Her goals were simple, to cook dinner for her husband and clean her home.

Suddenly Diane smiled her signature smile. She lit up the room. I had captured the moment she took her first step holding on to the railing, but you could see her hope and exhilaration about taking the next step and the next step. Any frustrations I felt about being away from my business (hey, keeping it real) for so many appointments faded away as I saw her take that first step. I felt so blessed to be part of this journey with her. Documenting every step, every emotion for her husband and family to see. Diane was adamant about documenting this process because her husband had no time left to take from work and they needed him to stay employed for the health insurance.

Often, we would follow these visits with lunch if Diane was up to it. That day she was not too tired to go to lunch. Her excitement stayed with her the rest of the day.

Driving home from the beach, I held on to that moment for the rest of the evening. I could see her smile, her first step as a closed my eyes to try and sleep.

When I opened my eyes the next morning, I looked at the calendar. It was Thursday, September 9, 2020. That meant yesterday was real, Diane was gone. Today the family would gather to plan out Diane's funeral. My heart was so heavy, and it took all my energy to get ready to meet everyone

Walking up to the front door I could not stop my tears. I was going to walk through the door and Diane was not going to be sitting on the couch waiting to welcome me. She was not there. She would never welcome me into her home again.

I could hear my nieces, brother-in-law, and little sister inside. I stepped into the house and felt relief seeing everyone and all the activity underway. Even though we were here for such a sad reason, I felt calmer than I had since yesterday morning. Again, due to COVID we were facing challenges and changes to Diane's funeral services.

I walked into everyone going through pictures for her celebration boards. Someone came across one of her wedding pictures and I heard the comment, "I forgot how beautiful and full of life she was at one time." I remembered thinking the same when I watched Diane one day as she was trying on an outfit for an upcoming event. I could see her closet filled with her professional and dress clothes from years ago. Scanning her clothes brought up so many emotions. I remember closing my eyes, struggling to remember the healthy, vibrant, professional woman she was for so many years. As I remembered that moment, I realized we needed to make sure her collages were not only about her illness but about her life. I went through pictures with everyone, desperate to find the right ones that really showed her energy, her spark all throughout her life. In the end my nieces did a wonderful job with the picture collages that celebrated their mom's entire life.

We had limited time to get ideas organized before they all had to leave to meet with the funeral parlor and church. As we made decisions, I found myself comparing Diane's funeral arrangements to my sister Bev's services. I kept hearing Diane saying she really loved Bev's services and how happy she was that everyone showed up to celebrate her life. It crushed me that Diane's would be much smaller. I could not shake this as the day wore on. It tore at me that another thing was being taking away from her because of COVID. My anger at the damn pandemic and the affect it had had and was having on my sister's life and her death grew.

When people left for appointments, I stayed behind to continue going through the photos. I wanted this time to go through childhood photos when "the Duffy Sisters" were still all together. Every childhood holiday picture showed all four of us wearing dresses, ruffles, white gloves, and hats. My mom loved to dress her girls up. One of my uncles once said, "No wonder the Duffy girls don't get in trouble; they can't move with all those ruffles." Smiling, I came across the first formal wedding of one of our cousins. No ruffles this time, but we were all in long gowns. The picture was of the four of us with Mom and Dad. I spent the few hours I had alone looking at hundreds of pictures, recalling hundreds of Duffy memories. For a brief moment, my heart was filled with pure love and joy.

The door opening startled me back from my walk down memory lane. Back to the ugly reality of the day. I could not believe when they told me her wake would be Friday night, the next day, and her mass on Saturday. They wanted to avoid having her services on the upcoming Monday. That would be Diane and her husband's nineteenth wedding anniversary. The rest of that day was a whirlwind of activity to have everything ready for tomorrow. I still could not stop comparing Diane and Bev's services. I hoped people would be there for Diane Friday and Saturday. When I heard all the restrictions in place at the funeral parlor and the church, my heart sank. I also felt like people did not have enough time to plan to attend. Nor was there adequate time to get notice to everyone. It was not right. Diane deserved a huge celebration. I was angry at the timeline. I was still fighting with COVID. I kept hearing Diane's comments about how so many people loved Bev and how happy she was they all showed up to say goodbye. I kept all these thoughts to myself. I drove home deflated and frustrated at how things were going to be. I fell asleep sad.

I awoke before the sun, restless. I grabbed my keys and headed to the beach. I sat there in rage. I could not believe I had to go through this again. The scene that played out before me did not help matters. Me and two of my sisters at three funerals burying our beloved sister Beverly, our dad, and then our mom. We were such a close family. We were known by everyone as "the Duffy's" not as individuals.

In just a few hours two sisters would stand in line at the services of another sister taken too soon in part because of family genetics, history, and lifestyle decisions. Rage continued bubbling up inside of me at all of them for dying, for not taking better care of themselves, for not growing old, and for leaving their children. This was not how it was supposed to be!

It pains me to admit this, but somewhere in my thoughts the words "who will be next" were playing along with questions. Would I die soon, too, because of a chronic health condition, illness, disease, or lifestyle? How do I break this cycle? How do I make sure my son does not lose his mother too soon? Will I be around to meet his wife, his children? This spiraled and elevated a recent fear I had developed. My fear of getting COVID had crippled me and forced me into isolation whether by a stay-at-home order or not. How would I deal with my fear today?

At that moment, an idea popped in my head. I had to find something good to offset COVID restrictions. A way to honor Diane. I found the perfect idea. It was a little thing I could do, but it was also a big statement in honor of something my sister loved.

I walked into the funeral parlor wearing a New England Patriots face mask to honor my sister. The entire family loved it and wished they had thought of it. It was too late for tonight, but I was on a mission now. I solicited the help of my little sister's husband to help me with my plan.

Diane's wake was a different experience than I was accustomed to. All the restrictions prevented people congregating, the fear people had of being in crowds kept some away, and the limited time we had to notify people resulted in only a small steady flow of people to pay their respects. To me something was missing. Traditionally people would linger, reminiscing about Diane's life and such. Not tonight. The only people allowed to remain in the room throughout her wake were family members selected to be in the receiving line. Even the number of family members in the receiving line was adjusted. There was no line of people waiting inside. There were no people sitting, just wanting to remain near Diane and us. People came in slowly with no more than five people able to be in the room with the receiving line at any time. Do not get me wrong, it was special and brought such comfort to me seeing all who came. It was the quietness and organized fashion in which it played out that took away something for me. Before too long, against protocol people were hugging, holding hands, and kissing so my fear of contracting COVID lingered all around me through the evening and for days afterwards. Leaving the services, I did not feel comforted, mostly discomfort.

People were forced to remain separated throughout this time when we would normally be together. Making the morning of Diane's mass seem like a normal day except for the sadness. There was no scrambling to get to someone's house to be together heading out for the mass as a family. It felt so separated to me. The only good thing was that my brother-in-law and I were able to pull together my idea.

The family gathered outside the church and waited while everyone went in. They were happy with my surprise. Diane was a huge New England Patriots football fan. Between my brother-in-law and me we found over twenty Patriots face masks for the entire family and pallbearers to wear as we walked down the aisle. As everyone adorned their masks, I could not think of a better way to turn a protocol of COVID into a unique way to add something Diane loved dearly into her celebration mass.

As the church doors opened and we all started the sad walk down the aisle you could see everyone's surprised look and smiling eyes, making us all stand a bit taller as we continued down the aisle, honoring Diane, a beloved wife, mother, sister, grandmother, aunt, friend, and Patriot's fan.

The priest knew of her love for the team and was able to incorporate it into the mass. Remembering this one simple act I could do for her would help me in the months to come. I know Diane was smiling down from heaven during her services.

After the services people congregated in the parking lot awkwardly. There would be no graveside service or celebrational lunch gathering for everyone. We just had a small luncheon planned for the immediate family. The services were intimate, comforting, beautiful, and filled with love. I cherish the memories of Diane's services. I still felt bad that many people could not be there, but I finally stopped comparing my two sisters' services.

I arrived home later that day with a realization about my grief process. My healing usually begins amongst the hundreds of people moving through the services providing comfort, love, and stories about my loved one. I did not get that healing this time. As I entered my home alone and closed the door, the weight of my grief scared me.

I became indifferent to what was happening in my life and business. I wish I had become indifferent about my COVID fears, but they continued to cripple me from doing public gatherings. The holidays were going to be tough. I needed to begin working on being comfortable with the family through the holidays. I began visualizing the holidays. I visualized me being happy participating in all the festivities. It worked so I added visualizing being healthy and COVID free. It worked; I was ready.

There were still crowd restrictions during the holidays. It was "strongly encouraged" to keep gatherings small. We did not gather as a complete family. Still, Diane not being with us created a sadness that hung in the air knowing she would not be at anyone's Thanksgiving dinner or rushing in for Christmas. Right before Thanksgiving my son tested positive for COVID, so I spent that day driving to their home to check on them and dropping food at the door. I stood outside, six feet away, longing to hug him. Christmas was the same, just a small group of the family gathered. The day was nice, but I did not have my usual enthusiasm. I was not concerned and thought it was normal, since we had just lost Diane.

I began getting concerned when it was almost a year, and I did not feel like I had made any progress with my anger and grief. I had barely left my apartment, comfortable living in a cocoon. My lifestyle became sedentary.

I learned I am a binge eater through grief. I had not fully reengaged with my business. I just did not care. I functioned but not at the level I normally function. I am a high energy, positive person. I always see the positive in everything. I desperately wanted to shift back to the vibrant me living my desired life but did not. I could not even bring myself to use any of the tools I knew would help me. I became a fraud trying to look like my life was fine. Faking my happiness, existing in my life not living my life. I engaged at the bare minimum acceptable. I faked it when I had to "be on" for people which exhausted me. Alone I thought, *what does it matter?* I was a robot going through the motions of my life.

One morning I looked in the mirror and something happened. I heard my gasp. Who was this in my mirror; it is not me, was it? It scared me. For the rest of the day, I held that picture of me in the mirror as I forced myself to take a hard look at what I had been doing. Or should I say, what I was not doing? When was the last time I smiled or truly laughed?

I took days, but I eventually pulled out all my tools, and this time I got to work implementing them. I started by thinking of something, anything to be grateful for each day. Over time I went from one grateful statement to two, three, and more. Looking at my calendar I noticed it was the end of July. A month away from my birthday. I took that as a sign and set that as the day to see significant improvement in my spirit and energy. To reengage with my life and especially my business. I spent the next thirty days asking questions of myself and documenting the answers and when needed, documenting the solutions in my journal. "I AMs" became part of my daily routine. Where I found a negative anything I began replacing it with a positive everything. I dove in and began lifting the fog around my life. I started remembering when I laughed, smiled, and felt something. It did not take long before I was spending more time rediscovering myself and less time in the pity party for one life I created.

I had quick discoveries that were surprising. My disinterest in life was not just about my sister's death. It was not just about my fear around COVID. A huge amount of my anger that I directed at COVID centered around my lifelong dream of seeing the US ripped out from under me just as it started. I am not ready to travel again but I have started developing an even bigger travel plan.

As I began to find my way back to me, I was handed a gift: theopportunity to receive coaching from an expert in human potential and business development. All I had to do was get to Florida. I again turned to visualizing to help release anything that would prevent me from leaving my cocoon and to start living boldly again. Amongst all the obstacles I needed to overcome the biggest was the date my session had been scheduled. I was to meet with him on September 8, 2021, one day before the one-year anniversary of Diane's death. I almost cancelled, but did not.

I felt I did not represent myself well during that visit. I am extremely grateful for the time with him and one other expert. I left with a list of action items designed to lift my business up. Later I would wonder if they were the right actions. I continued to gain clarity and reengage with my life and realized I did receive the right actions. It just took me time to jump in and start implementing them. That visit turned out to be a huge pivot for me.

During preparing for the trip and throughout the trip, I felt both my big sisters with me, encouraging me and what sometimes felt like physical pushes to keep going. They would whisper, "It's time for you to soar and get back to your dreams. You called this person into your life for this moment. Now go." The night before I was to have my session, I fell asleep to their whisper, "Remember what you always say, the best way to honor a loved one who died is to live fully. Live fully, sis." I still have not decided if those words were actually spoken to me or if I simply dreamed them. It did not matter because they were working.

It has been a little over seven months since I started my "reengage in life" plan with a little help from my sisters. I still have plenty of challenges to work on. Thankfully, I have more positive days than nonproductive days. My grief still runs deep. Tears are still part of my day. I feel my spirit, positivity, and dreams coming back. My business is back on track, and I am expanding it in new directions that are exciting. I wake up ready to face each day. I am closer to being ready to love 100 percent again. Most importantly I am honoring my sisters by working my way back to living fully!

CHAPTER 10

How Can Grief Lead to Joy?

In loving memory of Michael Patrick Barry
November 9, 1985 to April 5, 2012

by Barbara Barry

Icould feel my blood rushing from my head down to my feet as I sat on the side of our bed. What had he just said?

"I love you and I am always with you. God loves us and is always with us. Mike is no longer with us."

My husband, John, woke me shortly before my alarm time. "Barb, wake up. Wake up."

As I opened my eyes, he asked me to sit up and sit on the side of the bed next to him. Our son Mike had died quietly and peacefully during the night, succeeding at last in dying by suicide.

John and I went to our daughter Laura's room to tell her that her best friend was gone.

Together the three of us entered the dining room. Against the door was a binder, blocking the door into the family room. Propped against the binder was a note Mike had written. *He loved us very much and hated to leave us because it would hurt us so much. Yet he just couldn't continue living with his worsening mental illness and depression and had made several attempts in the prior few months.*

Mike was seated in a chair at the front end of the room. He was wearing a sleep mask, as he often did, which spared us from seeing his lifeless eyes. As I knelt before him, I put my arms around him and wept on his knees.

How thoughtful and kind he had been to us, *even in planning his death.*

His note, the sleep mask, and even choosing our own home—his safe haven—as the location.

Because it was clear Mike was gone, we didn't call 911 right away. In the next two hours, everyone going off to school and work would see the emergency vehicles. Mike wouldn't have wanted to create a stir. Instead, we had those hours to hug what was left of Mike and to weep, which was a great comfort to us. At some point, John removed my dad's rosary beads from Mike's hand. I believe that he had prayed, *"Hail Mary…pray for us now…at the hour of our death."*

My husband led Laura and me in the early hours of our grief journey. First, John had discovered Mike and had to tell us both. Next, he called two of our siblings, our employers, and our church. His taking charge of phone calls allowed me the chance to grieve sooner and more fully.

The fire department chaplain told us that Mike hadn't taken his life, but that his mental illness had done so. Later one of our parish priests consoled us with his message that God had made Mike this way, with this illness, so certainly God would welcome Mike home to heaven.

Our pastor, Father James Ruggieri, visited us later that day with more love and comfort. Truly this was a radical departure from the old days of the Catholic Church. Decades ago, the church would not offer a funeral mass nor burial in a Catholic cemetery to someone who had taken their own life. In more recent years, the church had embraced the more merciful and uplifting approach that we experienced following Mike's death.

Those familiar with Christian traditions will appreciate that Mike died on Holy Thursday, the day that celebrates Jesus' Last Supper. As we knelt before our lifeless son, we immediately knew some of the pain his mother Mary felt at the foot of the cross. *We were not alone in our agony.* Christians around the world would be in a state of mourning for the next few days, remembering Christ's suffering and death—we had company there too.

For the first three nights, John and Laura and I all slept in the living room, all needing the security of being in the same room together.

On Friday and Saturday, some nieces and nephews brought photos and scanners to our house. For hours, they scanned photos together, sharing memories and laughter, and creating three collage posters to display at

Mike's wake. They were a lively and loving presence when we so needed them!

Easter Sunday brought a different flavor of grief. The Christian world was now rejoicing in Jesus' resurrection from the tomb.

Not ready yet to see our friends at our own church and face questions, we attended Mass at another church. One of the priests at this church had been our pastor when our children were growing up. When the crowd had cleared after Mass, Father Halloran opened his arms and embraced all three of us in one big hug. With his long, loose, white garments, we felt like Christ was enfolding us in love.

Many people don't like the concept of a funeral wake, or "viewing of the body." We have attended many during our lives and had been the family at the wakes of John's and my parents. Never did I expect to be so comforted by the ritual as I was with Mike's wake. In the first room were the photo collages lovingly made by family, each collage full of precious memories. A video of photos played in the room where our son's body lay in the casket. This is also where people greeted us.

For many hours I barely moved outside of a four-foot-square area while we received our guests. We neither ate nor drank nor visited the restrooms—nor felt the need to. Some attending the wake shared stories of Mike as a teammate, fellow Scout, or student in their classroom. Others simply shared their love and offers of prayers for our consolation. One couple traveled fifty miles to attend on behalf of their son, a close friend of Mike's in college. We experienced especially poignant visits from his childhood doctor, who had saved him from pneumonia at age eight, and Mike's psychiatrist for the last five years. We credit this man with helping Mike to cope with life for five years longer than he would have otherwise.

Each person who came brought what seemed to us like a hug from God. Hearing how Mike had touched so many people's lives gave us great joy and comfort.

Mike's wake, funeral mass, and graveside service allowed us opportunities to receive and return God's love through the people around us, and to express our love for Mike and for God with those people. We chose readings and music that reflected our faith and trust in God, and we welcomed others to share our joy of gratitude to God for giving us Mike to love. We chose to walk beside the casket on the way up to the altar. Along with Mike's godparents and one aunt, Laura, John, and I each walked with one hand on the casket.

Through our tears we were smiling (!) as we brought Mike back to God. How was that even possible? We could never have imagined it.

Our Privileged Journey with Mike

As children, both Mike and Laura were lively and happy. Laura was one grade behind Mike, so they were the best of friends, together during most of grade school and middle school. They chose separate high schools yet happily reunited in college. During middle school, Mike became more rebellious, talking excessively in the classroom and skipping homework. At times, after a meeting with his teachers and guidance counselor at his school, I arrived at my Catholic elementary school just in time to slip into church, light a votive candle, kneel, cry, and pray. *What did Mike need from us? From me? From God? "Our Father...thy will be done..."* even though I didn't understand God's will. *"Hail Mary...pray for us NOW..."*

His first year in high school was terrifically successful. Academically and socially, he thrived with his involvement in marching band, track, and lacrosse. He was a Boy Scout, eventually rising to the rank of Eagle Scout in his senior year. We were so thankful that Mike was finding his way!

During tenth grade, he began to experience the onset of depression and social anxiety born of mental illness. He became more isolated, dropping out of activities at school. He met weekly with his Scout troop, and he hung out with a few friends from school who, like Mike, avoided the party scene. More prayers for guidance: *how did God want us to support Mike?* John and I took him for counseling during tenth and eleventh grades, and during his senior year he began psychiatric treatment, including medication.

This mental illness had turned Mike's world upside down. Our son who had always been so vibrant, talkative, and lively was now often subdued, silent, and sedentary. He didn't know what to do with his thoughts and feelings. Anything could trigger an angry verbal outburst or lengthy outpouring of hurt feelings about a perceived slight. He became very quiet in school, though at the dinner table, he could talk nonstop throughout the meal. At times he was gleeful, like his old self, yet we never knew what to expect. We celebrated his good days, and we suffered along with him on his bad days. It was very stressful and painful to have our whole family's wellbeing revolve around something that neither Mike nor we could predict or control.

We were all concerned about his going off to college, but he went anyway, a very long two hours from home. Beginning in his sophomore year, Laura was on campus too, and they shared many friends. He enjoyed many friendships and some academic success, although he just could not manage a full course load. Halfway through his junior year, he could no longer sustain his energy or focus for any courses at all. Was it attention deficit disorder (ADD)? The depression? The anxiety of working in a shared study room in his dorm? Or the loneliness of not feeling comfortable anywhere, yet needing to spend time outside his small dorm room? Or missing the comfortable setting of home? The day after second semester began, Mike came back home. He simply wasn't thriving, so he withdrew from school.

2007-2012—Anticipatory Grief

In February, Mike told my husband and me he was having suicidal thoughts. We took him to the hospital emergency room immediately. He was hospitalized for about a week. For the first time, he chose to let some extended family members know what he was enduring, and even to visit him in the hospital. Up to that point, only John, Laura, and I really knew. We carried that burden silently with Mike.

Two months later, in the middle of the day, he was angry and threatening to hurt himself. I called the police and had him arrested for his own safety. John called Mike and endured Mike's irrational, angry tirade. Then John told him, "Nothing you do or say can ever make me stop loving you." He was like the father in the Prodigal Son parable. Mike quieted down immediately and stayed calm as the police arrived. Mike's therapist at that time helped us to arrange for the court to release him to us, and to get him into our state's best psychiatric hospital that evening.

As we later learned from our grief therapists, in this phase of our lives, John and Laura and I were experiencing "anticipatory grief," anticipating that Mike was facing a long and painful illness.

Our lives felt completely chaotic, but it was the beginning of a period of recovery for Mike. He was in the hospital for two weeks and then participated in an outpatient day program. He was pretty good for a few more years. From that point Mike was under the care of a psychiatrist at Butler, who gave him the very best care. If not for that intervention, we would have lost our son at that time. He admitted himself to the hospital one more time, eight months before he died.

What Eased or Still Eases My Grief?

On the most fundamental level, I believe in a **loving and merciful God** who gave me this young man to love and cherish for twenty-six years on this earth. I believe that Mike is with God and still with us but in a different way, and someday our family will be reunited in God's presence.

I am grateful for the beautiful blessing of Mike in my life. I've expressed this prayer daily since he was a little boy. *"Lord, hold Mike close to you and help him become all that you will him to be. Thank you for the wonderful gift of Mike."* I pray the same gratitude prayer for Laura, and now for her family also.

Forgiveness. Mike expressed anger at God for many years for giving him the illness that kept him from reaching his potential in life. During the last seven months of his life, I believe that Mike forgave God. In those months, Mike and Laura had joined a Catholic young adult ministry, sharing faith, food, football, and friendship. This is how he came to be holding his grandfather's rosary beads during his final hours.

With many hours of Hail Mary's during birth labor, I had prayed Mike into the world. With the Hail Mary's of the rosary, I think he prayed himself into heaven.

Inspiration and role model. I knew there must be a way to find joy again. As a young woman, my mother had lost her younger brother in a flight school training accident, and six months later lost her fiancé in a car crash. Yet she was among the most joyful people I've ever known.

Family gathering 'round. In the evening of Mike's death day, many family members visited just to be together with us. A special visitor was a friend of ours who had lost his younger brother to suicide a year earlier. He shared stories of his brother's traits, and we all learned that our two young men had much in common—and that both were too gentle for this rough world.

Transitioning Mike's bedroom. Because Laura was leaving for graduate school four months after Mike's death, we decided as a family to take his bedroom apart while she was still at home. It would save her the trauma of returning at Thanksgiving to a home that didn't have her brother's room. We repurposed Mike's room as a den, a sacred place for prayer. Every item in the room was related to Mike and placed there for our consolation. When Laura came home for Thanksgiving, we followed her grief counselor's recommendation to return Mike's bed to the room so Laura could be consoled by sleeping there if she chose to. We didn't give away Mike's possessions immediately though, and we have kept many for ourselves. Over the first few years we shared some of his treasures with family members. Each giveaway led to another period of deeper grieving but gratitude from the recipient.

Rituals. Every day, I wear both a rosary bracelet and a black cord necklace with a pewter pendant: a cross with a large heart in the center. Laura and Mike had given me the necklace for Mother's Day when they were about seven and nine years old. While Laura was doing volunteer service 7,000 miles away in Rwanda, I started wearing it daily, because it represents my family, and I felt united with her. Yes, I prayed every day, *"Our Father...thy will be done,"* i.e., *"Please protect Laura while she's far from home."* Since losing Mike, I wear my heart-cross all the time. God is with my family, no matter what happens.

For years after converting Mike's bedroom, each morning I sat in

Grandpa Barry's armchair, which Mike had enjoyed in his room, for my prayer and meditation time. One of Mike's favorite sweatshirts was draped over the back of the chair, and two throw pillows sat on the chair. Sometimes I just hugged the pillows because they were connected to memories of Mike.

I continued my years-long morning routine of either swimming or exercise classes in the YMCA pool. I could pound water and kick until I had worn myself out. Many loving friends surrounded me there.

Gifts and cards. During the first few days and weeks after Mike died, many people brought or sent gifts of meals, fruit baskets, books, and cards. A few continued for several years to bring food over around Mike's birthday and anniversary. Some friends and family members send us cards, emails, or text messages on Mike's anniversary. Knowing that they remember the date helps us to grieve and to be thankful for Mike and for them.

Gifts of service. We were generously given many gifts of service as well. Just as his cousins had composed the photo posters, one helped us move Mike's furniture from his bedroom, and many other people stepped in to help us as they saw opportunities.

Near Mike's first anniversary, one very special student edited most of the yearbook herself, recognizing that I could not do the work. I am forever indebted to her! The project was fraught with awful memories of the prior year, when I had been completing both the yearbook and quarterly report cards. I literally had been too busy to celebrate my own birthday. Though Mike and Laura sang "Happy Birthday" to me in the early minutes of my birthday, we postponed the full celebration. Three days later Mike died, and it was several years before I felt worthy of celebrating my birthday again.

Mike's friends. For a few years, I kept up with Mike's friends on Facebook. I celebrated their birthdays, weddings, or first homes, congratulating them and sending love from Mike Barry's mom.

A group of Mike and Laura's friends from their young adult ministry came to visit on the day after he died. Every year on his anniversary, they have joined us or hosted us for dinner to remember and celebrate Mike and to share about their own lives. What a beautiful gift they are to us and to the world! We have met virtually since the seventh anniversary.

Grief counseling. Since my late thirties, I have taken medication for low-grade chronic depression and visited counselors many times.

The day after Mike's funeral, John, Laura, and I all made appointments with a grief counselor, to see her individually. I continued my visits with her for several years. She gave me valuable perspectives on my loss, my grief, and my transition in identity from mom to grieving mom to resilient grieving mom and suicide loss survivor. I could indeed find new meaning in life.

We learned from our counselors that for us, the shortest path to healing our grief was to turn directly into the emotional storm instead of running from it. Go into the dark places, our anger, frustration, regrets, and other negative feelings. That strategy worked well for us.

As our identities evolved, we would integrate our grief into our lives. Integrate it, make it a part of us, and not denying it or repressing it.

As Mike's illness affected him more deeply in his later years, John described our role as Mike's parents this way: we responded like the mother in the film *The Exorcist*, whose child was suffering (the daughter was possessed by the devil). When anyone in their right mind would run in the opposite direction, you get right onto the bed with your loved one, to be with them in their horror and torment.

According to our grief therapists, for the prior eleven years, as we saw Mike slowly become more shackled by his mental illness, we were experiencing anticipatory grief. Indeed, before Mike's death, my counselor had encouraged me to answer the question, *"What if he were successful?"* For years we had feared losing Mike's beautiful personality and intellect to a dim version of himself. During those years, he had undergone three stays in the psychiatric hospital, as well as ongoing talk therapy, psychiatric visits, and daily medication. (The exceptions were the several times when he stopped his medicine cold turkey without consulting his doctors, indeed flushing his medicine down the toilet.) Though we denied the possibility of a successful suicide attempt, during his last month Laura, John, and I all felt more anxious about him than ever.

Compassion. Other grieving parents whom we knew reached out to us, offering the chance to talk, sending their favorite books, and suggesting other resources. They shared our pain, and that helped ease ours.

During my first weeks back in school, while teaching at the front of the room, I sometimes felt tears running down my cheeks. On several occasions, one or another of the girl students came to the front of the room and gave me a great big hug. What beautiful hearts they showed!

Dozens of people whom I saw regularly asked "How are you doing?" and they waited and listened with open hearts.

Books. John read many books and shared the highlights with me. (See Emmaus Ministry below.)

Grieving a Suicide: A Loved One's Search for Comfort, Answers, and Hope by Albert Y. Hsu. In the western world, most people have come to assume that life will always turn out the way we planned, that we are entitled to live a life without suffering. Yet that's not what God promises.

Martha Whitmore Hickman's *Healing After Loss: Daily Meditations for Working Through Grief.* During the three or four years that we read it together daily, John and I kept extra copies on hand and often gave away our current copy whenever we learned of someone's fresh grief.

The Grief Quest Journal for Grieving Parents (Weinstock & Julien) includes a thirty-day journal with questions about your child's traits, what you miss most, what frustrated you about them, etc. It was very valuable to us, as we wrote our answers in notebooks and went through the thirty-day process two or three times.

Organizations. The Compassionate Friends (TCF) is an international organization for families who have lost a child of any age, a sibling, or a grandchild. The meetings permit an opportunity to share the pain of losing our own child and to connect with other families. TCF also has a national convention, held in Boston the year after we lost Mike. Some talks were titled *Grieving a Stigmatized Death* (suicide, shaken baby syndrome, gun accidents), *What to Do with Your Child's Possessions*, and *Grief Quest*.

Emmaus Ministry for Grieving Parents. I can't praise this program any more highly. Its day retreats deal with the spiritual aspects of grieving the death of a child. Since our first retreat, three years after losing Mike, we have participated in numerous EMFGP retreats, including in leadership roles. Within this ministry I experience the opportunity to support other grieving parents in profound ways. The organization's website includes a wonderful list of books, many of which we have read.

The Angel of Hope Garden in Sturbridge, Massachusetts. The angel statue here is a replica of one based on Richard Paul Evans' bestselling book, *The Christmas Box*. As we read the memorial bricks that honor deceased children, it felt like we joined hearts with hundreds of other grieving parents, soothing our shared hurt. It made me thankful that we had had Mike for twenty-six years. The garden overlooks a portion of a traditional Catholic Stations of the Cross, set in the hilly woods of St. Anne's Shrine. We couldn't help but compare Mike's suffering to that of Jesus on the way to his death. We returned on each Good Friday (Mike's informal anniversary) for many years.

Creating new traditions.

Thanksgiving. In the first year, after falling into an emotional valley at a Fourth of July party, we recognized that we could not possibly celebrate Thanksgiving and Christmas in our usual ways. At Thanksgiving, John, Laura, and I attended Mass in Narragansett, seeing our former pastor again, and then walked the town beach, warmed up at a coffee shop in town, and visited the cemetery. The first year we ate Thanksgiving dinner at a restaurant far from our town, among strangers. Each year we still follow our Narragansett and cemetery traditions.

Christmas. For the first two years after Mike's death, the three of us spent December 24-26 in a small inn in New Hampshire. It was peaceful, cozy, and snowy. As we had always done, we would celebrate Christmas with each side of our family during the week after Christmas. But for Christmas Eve and Day, we were just too emotionally raw to be with anyone, or to be alone in our house. Huddling and hibernating were very soothing.

Birthdays. As Mike and Laura were growing up, and even into adulthood, I always baked and decorated their birthday cakes. In 2012, on

Mike's first birthday after he died, *I needed to bake* in order to process my grief during his birthday week. My sister Mary, our friend Cheryl, and I baked and frosted about eighty cupcakes for all the students at the school where I was teaching. All in the cafeteria joined us in singing "Happy Birthday" to Mike. After the second year, Mary suggested simplifying to chocolate chip cookies—no frosting required! That's been our tradition ever since. Since I no longer teach in a school, I take the cookies to wherever I am going, whether a business meeting or the gym. Sometimes recipients tell me that they also have lost a child or dealt with mental illness in their family. My cookie tradition and telling my story helps others to share their sorrows more freely. I need to celebrate the gift of Mike!

Mike's anniversary/Good Friday. Anniversaries can be awfully hard. The first few, and bigger ones, like the tenth, were especially painful. Since the second year, we have focused most of our grieving energies not on Mike's actual anniversary but on Good Friday, because Mike died on a Holy Thursday. After discovering St. Anne's Shrine in Sturbridge, Massachusetts, on Mike's first anniversary, we made an annual Good Friday tradition of visiting there and praying the Stations of the Cross. After a time of contemplation in the Angel of Hope Garden, we went out to lunch before going home to rest. In Maryland now, we visit another shrine with outdoor Stations.

Other sources of comfort.

Music is a powerful element of my family's life. John and I met as members of a music ministry, and we always had some type of music playing in our home. In their early years, we woke Mike and Laura by playing a cassette of "Wake Up Toes" at the bottom of the stairs (or "Tarzan" or "Phantom of the Opera"). Each developed their own musical tastes, but we had many shared favorite artists and songs. After his death, any music of Mike's at first triggered tears and later became a comfort. On the other hand, sometimes I needed to cry but couldn't. Listening to my husband's playlist "Missing Mike" helped me to release those tears freely.

One of Mike's favorite songs ever was "The Luckiest" by Ben Folds. It offers a profoundly wise perspective on life, set to a lovely, understated melody. "I love you more than I have ever found a way to say to you." We refer to it as Mike's anthem, and we never hear it except when one of us plays it on our phones. And except one day in 2018, six years after losing Mike. Laura had invited John and me to help her shop for her wedding gown. In a small bridal shop, she found it, and moments later, an instrumental version of "The Luckiest" played on the store's playlist. We knew immediately that Mike was with us, and that he was delighted for his sister. We wept—with sorrow and with joy.

Language. Our shorthand language of grief, which John, Laura, and I express aloud or in text messages: *Missing Mike. I'm "griefy" (Laura invented the word). I'm raw (emotionally) or I'm low. I'm feeling off.*

Regrets. I have no regrets. We (John, Laura, and I) love Mike fully and unconditionally, as we did when he was alive. He knew it and acknowledged it, and he loved us thoroughly too. We gave him the best care that we could, and he worked as hard as he could to stay healthy.

Signs. I always listen and watch for signs from Mike: a familiar song, a beautiful car, a rainbow, or a hawk or eagle soaring overhead. These signs make me happy.

Hugs—physical, socially distanced, or even virtual—are a powerful way to express my caring and concern for other people, and a great comfort to receive from others. Placing my hand over my heart conveys my joy, concern, or prayers. Receiving such a gesture is very soothing to me.

Focus. Focusing on other people's needs helps me to forget my own grief for a while.

What to say. "What would you like me to know about Mike?" This is the most significant question anyone can ask me about my grieving. Mike was good, kind, and faithful, with gorgeous blue eyes and a hearty laugh.

"On a scale of one to ten, what's your grief level today?" I have learned to ask that question of myself and of others, because sometimes I can't figure out why I am feeling a certain way. It's okay to cry! Indeed, it's good and necessary for body and soul.

Forgiveness and openness. I work hard at forgiving people who say awkward things or avoid asking about Mike, for fear of triggering my tears. I've made the same errors because I just didn't know what to say. When people ask how I am coping with my son's death, or how I can go on living, I answer them openly, and I conclude with *"Thanks for asking."* Being asked is so much more comforting than being ignored.

Fatigue. Grief is exhausting! During *griefy* periods, like near Mike's birthday or anniversary, I give myself permission to rest more, take time for myself, and go to bed early.

Boundaries. Sometimes grief has to be delayed, so I can focus on something that I must do right now. When a trigger sets off the grief alarm, or grief starts welling up like a drumbeat, I acknowledge it and schedule time that day or that week to immerse myself and engage with it.

Life After Mike's Death

Six years later: Laura is engaged to marry Joe, the love of her life.

Seven years later: Laura and Joe's wedding on a spring Saturday in 2019. Our family grows!

John and I could not love Joe more if he were our own child, and Mike would surely love him as a brother. That Laura and Joe found each other and love each other is a glorious blessing. Just as Joe fits seamlessly into our extended family, Laura meshes perfectly with Joe's parents and his three brothers. John and I have gained another whole family—Joe's!

Prior to the wedding weekend, John, Laura, and I spent Thursday evening together to contemplate, to remember Mike, and to cry. We didn't know what might trigger our tears at the rehearsal and dinner or on the wedding day. We celebrated the wedding mass at the church where Laura and Joe had met and were active members. Their reception tent overlooked the Chesapeake Bay, across an inlet from Joe's sailboat. They had thoughtfully prepared a table displaying photos of deceased loved ones: Mike, Joe's uncle, and all of Joe's and Laura's grandparents. Many guests remarked about feeling the poignant, palpable aura of love. It was a magical and miraculous celebration of love and of hope. An expected thunderstorm inexplicably detoured to avoid the reception. How blessed was that?

Eight years later: Our major move.

A few months after Mike's death, Laura had moved off to grad school and then to the Washington, DC, area. In Mike's absence, we missed Laura all the more, and we recognized that we needed to see her and Joe at least every few months. It was simply hard to breathe without the fresh air of their company.

Four months into the US' pandemic lockdown in 2020, John and I were extremely frustrated by our inability to visit them. Because many states had closed their borders, our plans to visit them for Easter were dashed. We lived in Rhode Island, the smallest state, and they lived a seven-hour drive away. They had just bought their first home in Maryland. We solved the problem by moving to Maryland ourselves.

In August, two weeks after our decision date, Joe and Laura were finally able to visit us. During that stay, they learned that they were expecting their first child. At the two-month mark, we spent our last night in the house where we had lived as a family of four, and where Mike had died. Four months after our decision, we enjoyed Thanksgiving dinner in our new home, near our kids and our future grandson.

Nine years later: A new life in our family.

On the ninth anniversary of losing Mike, John and I met virtually with his and Laura's friends from the young adult ministry, the same young people who had opened their hearts to us and annually celebrated Mike together. Laura and Joe were unable to meet that evening because they were in the hospital delivery room. Their son, Jack, arrived that night, on Mike's ninth anniversary.

John and I are relishing the opportunity to begin a new life in Maryland. Moving here, we jolted ourselves out of our comfort zone! After forty-plus years with our Rhode Island driver's licenses, we had to apply for Maryland driver's licenses. We are exploring new places, adjusting to the traffic patterns, and learning to use the DC metro. We have found a church community and joined a gym, both of which feel like home now. Although I will always love and miss my Rhode Island friends and family, we know that we are in the right place, near our Laura and her family.

> Love is patient, love is kind…It bears all things, believes all things, hopes all things, endures all things. Love never fails. (13 Corinthians, Catholic Bible)

Up until Mike died, my life was pretty blessed, darn near perfect, some might say. All four of our parents had died in their seventies and eighties, as is the natural order of life. When our parents died, I felt like a walnut that was cracked open. When Mike died, that walnut was sledge-hammered to smithereens. I have grown so much that, astonishingly, I am a better person because of losing my son.

With my husband and our daughter, I have learned that we can endure anything, and that we can rediscover hope and joy.

Seeing the radical joyfulness with which I live my life, most people would not imagine that grief is also an integral part of me. God loves us and is always with us. My ultimate mission in this life is to share God's love in the world, to shine his light in the darkness. I know that Mike is cheering me on. With all my loved ones and the wonderful son who left us too soon, I am—and we are—the luckiest.

CHAPTER 11

Our Love is Eternal

In loving memory of Nathan E. Cottrell
June 23, 1988 to March 9, 2017

by Susan Lataille

My life changed forever on March 9, 2017 at 4:04 a.m. with the last breath of my son. A part of me; gone forever. That part will always and forever remain with Nathan. What now? I had to figure out how to continue to live my life without my son and only child. I believe that our relationship and connection continues only in a much different way. I still need and want to feel that connection. My belief is that it is eternal.

Our story begins on June 23, 1988 at 10:55 p.m., the time my son was born in Rota, Spain. I was married while I was serving in the US Navy. Shortly afterward I was thrilled to be pregnant and was discharged while my new husband finished his tour of duty. Nathan was born on the naval base, which started our very special journey of almost twenty-nine years together.

I never thought I could love anyone this much! This boy was such a gift; he was so very special to me. This was the first time my life was changed forever in an instant. I was amazed at the age of twenty-two that I actually gave birth to this incredible child. I spent the first six months with him at almost every moment of our lives. I felt a special connection to him that I knew would last forever.

His life started off struggling with colic. Being an infant and new mother was a challenge for both of us. Plus, we were in Spain with no family or friends for assistance. I was grateful that one of my sisters came to visit us during that time to help. At moments I wasn't sure what to do or how to help him. As he grew out of the colic phase, he became a truly happy child. He was always smiling! Once he started walking there was no stopping him. All he wanted to do was go, go, go until he finally collapsed into sleep wherever he was at the moment. Sleeping always came easy to him and remained that way throughout his life. He could literally sleep anywhere including the floor! Most nights I was carrying him off to bed.

At the early age of two and a half, his father and I decided to a mutually acceptable split and divorced a year later. This was so difficult for him as he wanted to be with both of us. I remember each time upon returning from a visit with his father I would hold him in my arms as he would cry. I felt everything he did, so I cried along with him. This was one of the first times I wished that I could take his pain away. My heart broke for him every time and continues to when I think of his suffering.

His dad was a career Navy man and spent many years living in Virginia Beach. He would visit his dad and family on holiday weeks and vacations. Nathan started flying at the age of five. I'll never forget the first time he flew. The flight attendant took his hand, he said goodbye, and then went without turning back. Every time he left, I cried. I'd stand in the terminal until his plane left the gate and took off. I would talk to him as often as possible while he was away. This pattern continued until the age of thirteen. Due to many circumstances with school and classmates, we all decided—my son, his dad, and I—that he would live with his dad and go to school in Michigan.

His father had since retired from the Navy and went back to his home state. That was an extremely difficult decision to make. I wanted to do what was best for him, not for me. As it would turn out I was able to spend more quality time when he did visit me on holidays and vacations. We remained in contact talking at least once a week. I missed him so much while he was gone. It was like a piece of me was missing. I think he was starting to prepare me for living without him.

There's always been such an incredible bond between us. I was so proud when he graduated from high school. It was a tough road for him being diagnosed with attention deficit hyperactive disorder (ADHD) at the age of six. Sports helped him get through school. He always loved sports, playing and watching. It gave him something to focus on and a way to burn off energy.

Nathan continued to be a truly happy child through his teenage years. Loving all sports, he participated in as many as possible. His favorite were soccer and hockey. He also loved spending time with family and friends. He was very affectionate towards those he loved. Even with my parents who you could clearly see were uncomfortable when he hugged them and told them that he loved them.

While I questioned being a good mother many times, I do know that I loved him more than life itself. I would have done anything for him. If I could be with him now, I would go without hesitation.

After graduation Nate struggled with keeping jobs. Since school wasn't for him, he decided not to go to college. It just wasn't in the picture. He would bounce back and forth between Rhode Island and Michigan. He worked several landscaping jobs while living with me and then in the off-season would go back to stay with his dad. It remained hard for him to choose where he wanted to be. He had family and friends in both locations. Everywhere he went everyone loved him. He had a huge heart and was always aware of everyone's feelings and would have given the shirt off his back if asked. He put others before himself even in the end.

There was about a two-year period that I didn't see him. He was having a really difficult time finding a job in Michigan, so he and his girlfriend decided to go to Key West, Florida where her parents lived. He managed to find a job at a local hotel although barely making ends meet. His girlfriend broke up with him, making life more difficult. Occasionally, he would call and ask for money so that he could eat. My heart was breaking. Again, I wanted to take away his pain. Finally, on persistence from his father, he returned to Michigan after a year. I was happy to hear that he would have the support of his family knowing his struggle.

Leading up to his diagnoses, in April 2014 he came back home to me because his dad and stepmother didn't know how to cope with him anymore. He was extremely confrontational and unreasonable. Upon returning home I could clearly see that there was something wrong. He wasn't the affectionate, loving, and respectful son I knew. He continued to struggle with finding and keeping a job. He had no drive to do anything and was sleeping a lot.

I knew he was in pain. I thought that maybe it was because of his teeth. He did go to an urgent care once and they gave him pain medication that only made his aggression skyrocket. After he took them for a few days I managed to get to the bottle and put it down the garbage disposal. He was furious! And I was at my end. I just didn't know what to do or think at this point. I knew he needed help and I didn't know how to help him. He refused to go to the doctors. One of his friends actually brought him to the emergency room one night and he refused treatment. Apparently, he was having minor seizures that no one realized.

On November 7, 2014, my husband and I were getting ready to leave for vacation for a week on Cape Cod. I had continued to strongly suggest that he go to the doctors. He was afraid to know the outcome. Before I left that day, I said to him, "I don't know what's going on with you, but if you won't do it for yourself, please do it for me." That night he had a seizure while driving on a side street and hit a few cars. Gratefully, he wasn't hurt in the accident. When the police arrived, they transported him to the hospital not knowing what was wrong with him. He didn't remember much of what happened when I questioned him weeks later.

At 2 a.m. the following morning, I received a phone call from Johnston police, saying that my son was in an accident, and I needed to call the nurse at Woonsocket Hospital. When I spoke to the nurse, she told me that they found a large mass on his brain through a CAT scan. They would be transporting him to Rhode Island Hospital as soon as possible. I was in complete disbelief and wasn't even sure what I was supposed to do. I know now that I was in shock! I relayed the conversation to my husband and then called my brother (who stays up late and I've always been very close to) to tell him what had happened. I then laid down attempting to absorb what I was just told. After only a moment, I jumped up saying, "We need to go." We packed up, loaded the car, and made it home in record time.

On the ride home, I was not sure what to think. My thoughts raced to so many possibilities and outcomes including that my son wouldn't see his next birthday. He was only twenty-six years old. How could this be happening? I remember thinking before this happened that I was grateful for not having experienced any tragedy in my life up to now. Boy did this make up for it!

When we arrived at the hospital, he was so sedated and having seizure after seizure. I couldn't believe his condition. I did my best to comfort him by talking softly and touch his arm or leg. I so wanted to take away his pain. I wanted this nightmare to be over! I wanted to hold him and make everything better. My inside were torn apart while I kept a strong outside presence.

The doctors kept running different tests and finally did an MRI. I was grateful they let my husband and I go into the waiting area. Once the MRI was complete, we were told to go to the sixth floor waiting area and they would get him settled into a room. Again, I was standing in the waiting area not sure what to think or feel. I was ready to scream! I hated every moment I wasn't by his side.

My husband decided to go home at that point to shower and eat. I was alone and scared to know what was next. Being alone made my thoughts go in all different directions again. The surgeon came to see me and explained that Nathan needed to go in for emergency surgery and he was pulling a team together. It was about 5 a.m. on Saturday morning so his staff was off for the weekend. He also told me that he would treat him as if he was his own son and gave me a hug. I was touched by the compassion of his surgeon. I'll never forget his kindness at one of the worst moments of my life.

I was so grateful how everything happened, knowing that so many different scenarios could have changed everything. If the tumor continued to grow undetected it would have killed him instantly.

Next, I had to call his father in Michigan. I didn't even have his phone number. Strangely enough, it turned out my brother had it from many years ago. That was such an odd call, very awkward. I didn't even recognize Ed's voice when he answered the phone. It had been so long since I'd spoken to him. When I asked for him, he wanted to know who was calling. I replied, "Nate's mother." Then I proceeded to give him as many of the details as I recalled. I was in disbelief that all of this was happening and the words that were coming out of my mouth! All I could think was that I needed to be strong for everyone else. I tend to put everyone else before attending to my own needs.

He went into surgery, and I went home to shower before returning to the hospital waiting area. I sat there scared of the outcome until the surgeon came to tell us how it went. The minutes felt like days. Finally, the wait was over; his surgery was successful although the entire tumor couldn't be removed due to the location. We could go up to the sixth floor waiting area until he was settled into a room.

I was so grateful that he was strong. It was still so hard to believe that he just went through brain surgery. He was still sedated when we were able to go to his room. It took most of the day for him to become conscious somewhat because he was given so much pain medication. When he woke up and first saw me, he was so upset that I wasn't away on vacation. He was thinking of my needs as I was only thinking of him.

He pulled through that surgery with flying colors. It was amazing how quickly he recovered. His dad and stepmother arrived early the day after his surgery. It was strange seeing this man and his wife after many, many years. My son called her "Mom," as he had known her since he was three years old. I gave them the space to spend the time with him as he was recovering in Neurology ICU. He was able to come home after only a few days to continue his recovery. He was still so full of life.

The next two and a half years where up and down as Nate went through treatment and recovery, visiting his dad as he was able then returning for doctors' appointments and other services to me. It was so hard to witness him going through chemotherapy and radiation. My sweet boy was hardly recognizable due to the effects of the tumor and surgery except when he texted me. We texted every single day that he wasn't with me in the morning and at night. I still keep a copy of the text messages. In his message I could feel a glimpse of that sweet boy I've always known. Occasionally, I revisit those messages. I miss him so much!

God definitely has a sense of humor, as I'm very holistic in nature to have to watch my son go through the mainstream medical craziness. I believe in my heart that he came home to me because I allowed him to go through his process, as he needed, without interfering. I had to honor his wishes even when it conflicted with my own beliefs. I incorporated holistic modalities when it was possible to support his journey. I needed to feel that I was doing all I could in order not to have any regret.

I wanted Nate to start thinking about the future. He mentioned going to school a few times, but I think it was just to appease me. I believe that he knew he wouldn't be around much longer. He wanted to spend as much time as possible with those he loved.

He was good at telling everyone what he or she wanted to hear except for me. He knew that I was the one person that he didn't have to pretend. I remember questioning why he was so different in front of some people. I realized that he was showing them what they wanted to see while hiding what was really going on. When he was home, he would relax into how he really felt.

Having a full-blown seizure on July 4, 2016 while in Michigan was the first sign that his tumor had started growing again. His father experienced what it was like being with him in the hospital. He could be a handful. When I saw his stepmother calling me, I went into instant panic. I was a mess waiting for a report from the emergency room. He was so far away from me. Surprisingly, the CAT Scan didn't show anything, so he remained in Michigan for two more months.

Upon having an MRI when Nate returned home in September, the results showed that it had grown to a sizable tumor once again. He was deflated. After he received the results, it was one of those rare moments when he allowed me to hug him. He expected to go back to Michigan at the end of the month. He was so disappointed. I hated what this disease was doing to him. I hated not being able to help him.

Going through all the motions preparing for the second surgery was grueling. He had many doctors' appointments, test, pre-operation, etc. His second surgery was just about two years to the day on November 15, 2016. The anticipation was unlike anything I had experienced yet. Inside I was beyond worried. It was so much different this time as we were all prepared. The surgery went great although again the surgeon wasn't able to remove the entire tumor. It also affected his speech in a way that the words just didn't come out the way he was thinking them. This was very frustrating for him that he stopped talking unless he really needed to.

Upon receiving the pathology, we learned that he now had stage four cancer called glioblastoma. It's an aggressive type of cancer. We looked at all options including radiation and chemotherapy so he could decide on the best course of action for him. I presented him with all the options and let him decide. I continued to want this to be his journey. He started treatment shortly afterwards. Everything seemed to move so slowly.

Within six weeks I could see that Nate was starting to decline and asked for an MRI. An MRI couldn't be schedule without first seeing his oncologist. It took several weeks to get an appointment, then several more weeks to get an MRI, and a few more days to get the results. I was frustrated that so much time was going by between appointments. Nate was declining quickly.

Finally, at a last resort, I found a company in California that sold cannabis. They had great results with different types of cancer including the same diagnoses as my son. I had hoped it would help him as well. As it turned out, nothing I did helped him. He steadily declined despite all the different modalities I tried. Starting at the end of December, each week he declined more. He started to lose weight and forget things. It was so hard to watch as he forgot how to use the remote control and completely stopped using his phone. He used to always be listening to music or texting friends. I stayed patient and explained how to use things.

About two weeks before he passed, I was finally able to get some services in the home. I wish his doctors had given me this information sooner. I had no idea that he was eligible to receive in-home care. I finally had to call to request additional services. I was grateful for the help.

By the end of February, I was completely exhausted. I had been working from home in the morning before I got Nate up. I would let him sleep until about 11 a.m. before having him come upstairs to eat. By this point I would have to get him dressed and help him up the stairs, as he wasn't able to do it on his own. Most of the time I didn't even think about what was happening, as I was only focused on what needed to be done. About this time my husband asked me, "How long are you going to do this?" My reply was, "As long as I need to." It didn't matter at this point. All I could think of was caring for him.

I wanted to support him in all ways so I created a GoFundMe account to help with cost of holistic modalities that his health insurance wouldn't cover. The response was incredible. I appreciated every donation that was given. This allowed me let go of some of the money worries. Also, at this time one of his uncles was planning a fundraiser to help him. I was so very touched so many wanted to help.

Three days before his passing I invited a shaman friend to do a journeying session with drumming at our home. I hoped that it would benefit

Nate in some way. I had asked him several months before and he was so against it. That morning I let him know what was happening. I thought he would just want to stay downstairs. As it turns out, I went to check on him before my friend arrived and he was standing in his room. I hadn't seen him stand on his own in weeks. I was shocked! I said, "Okay, let's get you dressed and upstairs for some breakfast." I reminded him again that my friend Colleen was coming. If he wanted to go back downstairs, he would have to let me know. She arrived, I introduced him to her as he was finishing his breakfast. I was pleasantly surprised that he sat there absorbing the energy and the vibration of the drumming. I tried to relax but all I could think of was how he was doing. I kept opening my eyes to watch him. Colleen left immediately afterwards saying that she would call me.

A few hours later Colleen told me that Nate was 60 percent over on the other side although still undecided if he wanted to stay or go. Also, she said his aura appeared to be blueish liquid. It was something she had never seen. I wasn't sure what to think about what she told me. I wondered if it was possible he would stay. I prayed that he would stay.

That night, as I was putting him to bed, I told him that I loved him. His response, usually the only thing he said throughout the day was, "I love you, Mom." He just stared at me. I left him disappointed. I came back a while later before going to bed. I needed to change him and when I was finished again, I told him I loved him. I was so happy that he responded. It was the last time he spoke to say, "I love you, Mom." I'll forever be grateful that those were his last words.

The next morning, Nate wouldn't open his eyes. I had a really a difficult time getting him up the stairs because he wasn't able to help. The CNA bathed him and got him dressed all while he had his eyes shut. We sat him in the chair. He seemed to know I was there but wasn't able to respond. Shortly after the CNA left, I received a call from his nurse. She told me that his non-responsiveness was indicating something was seriously wrong and to call 911. I went into an instant panic as I did what I was told. I immediately called my husband to let him know what was happening and texted his father and stepmother. I was shaking as they loaded him into the back of the rescue. I was instructed to get in front. Was this really happening?

We arrived at the hospital, answered a series of questions, and then waited. The hospital staff did their thing and then he headed off to have an MRI. His surgeon came to see me as we were waiting for Nate to come back from his MRI. He gave me a hug and mentioned that he noticed that I lost weight during the course of being Nate's caregiver. The compassion of this doctor was comforting. It turned out his tumor had grown to the point where it was putting so much pressure on his brain that it was affecting everything. They gave him medication to help relieve the pressure. At about 8 p.m. was the last time he opened his eyes for a short time. I was happy to see his beautiful eyes once more. I smiled for the first time all day.

The next day was so tough. He was having seizure after seizure. Nothing the hospital staff was doing seemed to be helping. I kept asking the nurses if they could do anything for him. Finally, later in the day, I asked my husband to bring me his cannabis. I started to give him small doses. That seems to help him settle.

Earlier in the day I had asked a friend who's a minister to come and give him his last rights. I knew that it wouldn't be much longer. The timing couldn't have been more perfect as she arrived moments after Nate's father and stepmother left for the night. It was simple and appropriate for him. She always came up with the perfect words.

I settled in to stay for the night with him until they moved another patient into his room. The noise was unbearable to get any kind of rest. Finally, at about 11 p.m., I decided to go home to get some sleep. I asked the nurse on duty to call me if anything changed. At that time, he seemed to be comfortable and stable.

After sleeping only a few hours the phone startled me awake at about 3 a.m. I held my breath as I answered. It was the hospital telling me that I needed to come back as his breathing had become labored. I called his dad and headed back to the hospital fearing this could be the end.

Upon arrival, the nurse asked me if they had permission to make Nate comfortable, which meant morphine. I then sat on his bed with my hand on his heart. I spoke to him softly, telling him how much I loved him knowing that the time was near. After about twenty minutes, he took one last breath. It was so loud it scared me. I had no idea he would go that quickly.

I sit there for a few more minutes wondering if he was actually gone. His father and stepmother walk into the room a few minutes later disturbing my special time. I left the room to give them some private time with him. As I walked up to the nurse's station, the nurse on duty asks me if I knew he was gone. My reply was I wasn't sure. I asked her the time of death. Her reply was 4:04 a.m. That sounded like a special number to me.

I then had to walk back into the room to tell his father and stepmother that he was gone. I was in disbelief. I delivered the message, his father broke down, and his stepmother said, "But he's still warm." I waited around a few more minutes and then left them to have some time alone. In hindsight I wish I had stayed a bit longer. I was thinking that he was gone so there was no need to stay. The nurse asked if I was okay to drive home. I replied yes. I was relieved for him that he no longer had to suffer and heartbroken at the same time. "Is this real? How is this possible"?

I left the hospital in disbelief—*how could this be happening? How could he be gone?* I arrived home and my husband looked at me knowing that he'd passed before I told him. He held me although I wasn't able to break down. I thought I needed to be strong. A part of me was relieved that I didn't have to watch him suffer any longer. I also felt guilty for the relief. He had been through so much over the past five or six years. The other part of me would have taken care of him forever.

I attempted to get some rest knowing that I wouldn't be able to even though I was exhausted. A little bit after 7 a.m., the phone rang. It was New England Donor wanting to ask me questions about my son because, unknown to me, he had registered as an organ donor. It seemed so surreal talking about him as I answered a series of questions that went on for about twenty minutes. I was proud of my son that he had offered his organs to help others. Even in death he was thinking of others. His corneas were taken which gave two other people sight and a better quality of life. It warms my heart to know that a part of him lives on. His eyes were beautiful. Even on his last day of life, a nurse commented on his eyes.

I was amazed at how I could no longer feel his energy. His room felt cold, and it hurt so much not being able to feel him. This was so unexpected for me. The realization that he was gone hit me so hard. I didn't know how to continue living without him.

Somehow, I went through the motions of the day, asking my husband to call the funeral home, going to the appointment, and making his final arrangements along with his father. I was grateful that he gave me the freedom to do what I thought was best. I wanted to have a celebration of life after he was cremated. Thank God for the fundraisers that helped pay for his final expenses. I didn't have to worry about the money along with grieving.

The following Saturday, I invited my family over for lunch. Part of my process was to start cleaning out Nate's things. I held onto only the ones that were special to me: clothing, his first teddy bear, and a few other items. I gave my family things that I thought they would want. I gave clothes to my nephew along with coffee syrup and wipes along with other items to one of my sisters with small children. I thought if I was able to remove some of his belongings that it would somehow remove some of the pain. Unfortunately, it didn't work!

I wasn't sure what to do or say. I wasn't sure how to act. I wasn't sure if I could continue without him. I know a piece of me died with him that day. I know that we'll always be connected although that doesn't change the fact that I can't hold him or see him.

His celebration of life was held the following weekend. I was grateful to all those who came and again my friend for being the minister. As I welcomed his loved ones to speak, his father went first, followed by my brother, my sister, my son's aunt, and then, while I didn't think I was going to say anything, I felt like "how couldn't I?" after hearing everyone else.

I thought I was able to say exactly what I wanted. Saying that I learned so much more from him than he ever did from me. That we bring our children into this world thinking that we're going to teach them everything and in the end it's us that learns so much. His father used my exact words at his celebration of life in Michigan the following month.

I went through the motions of the day. Being strong and holding up well. I was still thinking that I need to be strong. I didn't know how to allow myself to be comforted by anyone. I was the one comforting others. I didn't cry through the service. I was strong! I could handle it! Boy, was I wrong!

The following month we drove to Michigan to attend Nathan's

celebration of life for his family and friends there. He had touched so many people's lives in both places. Up to attending the celebration, I thought that I was doing okay until I spent time in the energy of sadness once again. It put me right back. We didn't stay too long at the service. It was nice to see pictures that I've never seen before from his life there. It was touching and heart felt. One of my ex-sisters-in-law welcomed me to the club, a group of women who lost a child. I didn't want to be part of any group. I wanted to process this on my own. I didn't want to admit that I needed anyone else to help me.

In the beginning, I felt lost in my grief. I felt like I didn't fit in or belong anywhere. All I could think of while I was around other people was how different I felt. It was hard to watch others and have conversation that I now thought were superficial. I looked at life in a much different way. The trivial things in life just didn't matter. I finally understood not to sweat the small stuff!

I learned so much about myself through the caregiving and grieving process. It opened my eyes in so many ways. The first thing I learned was true love and compassion for another human being on such a deep level. I have an understanding of why compassion is necessary for everyone no matter where they are in their lives or what they are going though.

Asking for help was another huge lesson. I never wanted to have to ask because I had thought it made me weak. What I thought was, "I am strong." Even the strongest of us need help at times. We are not meant to do it alone. I had to find that sense of community again, a feeling like I belonged. Community is meant to help one another. I was too focused on not feeling like I belonged instead of looking where I fit in. Eventually, I found my tribe.

It always amazes me how you attract similar people into your lives. After the passing of my son, I met dozens of other women who also lost a child, mostly sons. It helped meeting these women as I had the chance to talk about my son and our story while listening to theirs. I have found that it's so important to speak of our loved ones and remember the happy moments. So often we focus on the tragedy of the loss whether to illness, an accident, or suicide. It took me several years to focus on the good memories when my son's suffering comes to mind.

I learned how gratitude is so important to me. It was the first thing I focused on to get me through those early stages. I was grateful that he came home so I could care for him. I can't imagine if he would have stayed in Michigan through his illness. I think I would have moved there! Next, I'm grateful for his last words—"I love you, Mom." In the end it filled my heart to hear those words each night when he would be silent during the day. He would give me a thumbs up or down when I asked him questions. Or he would give me this look that only I would know what he meant. We have such a powerful connection. Lastly, I was grateful to have the honor of being the only one in his hospital room when he passed. The list could go on and on. These are my top three.

Journaling has been helpful when needed. I learned that I could easily communicate with him through writing while speaking to him. After asking him a question, I would then get an answer. I was also able to do this by speaking. I hear his answer in my mind. I believe that it's him speaking to me.

The best memory I have of this is when I decided to go to Cape Cod for a few days when I just wasn't able to be around anyone. On the ninety-minute drive I went on a rant of why's: Why did he have to go? Why did he have to suffer? Was there anything else I could have done to help him? Did we choose the wrong course of treatment? Did he have the mental capacity to make that decision? I asked so many questions as the tears flowed done my face. I heard him say, "Stop, Mom, everything happened just the way was meant to. I was meant to go! I appreciate all that you did for me. I know that it wasn't easy." His words stopped me from continuing to go down that rabbit hole.

Getting out in nature has also been a blessing. It gives me a chance to clear my head. I have full out conversation with myself and sometimes with Nate. I love the beauty of nature and all it has to teach us. It's amazing what we can learn from Mother Nature when we stop to think about it. Resiliency is at the top of my list.

As I was processing my grief, I also sabotaged myself with large consumptions of wine in the evenings. I felt by nighttime, I just needed to numb myself. When anyone said something about it, I just said it was part of my grieving process. As it turns out after a few years, yes years, my body revolted. I got really sick after a weekend with some friends and drinking my fair share that I just couldn't stomach wine. My body said enough. I had no choice but to listen at this point. I still tend to go to alcohol when I'm in that space of grief or feeling down.

As the years passed along my grief journey I learned to give myself grace and allow the process. I'm able to give myself permission to grieve in my own way. We all are so different so why wouldn't we grief differently? At any moment that wave can hit like it just happened yesterday. That wave comes and goes in between the moments of happiness. Sometimes it's a calm wave and other times it's a tidal wave. Then there's every size in between. I've learned to go with the flow and live alongside grief. I found this is so important in healing. Healing is a process, layer by layer we heal and learn to enjoy life again. Also, that grief is not linear. There's no predetermined process, timeline, etc. to follow.

It's okay not to be okay! We live in a world where grief is so misunderstood. Unless you experience it yourself there's no way to understand. We're not meant to understand. When we dare to love deeply, we also grieve deeply. I wouldn't change anything in my experience of being Nate's mother. I'll always be his mother. Love is eternal. Our love is eternal!

"Why am I here?" was a question I asked over and over. What was the point? It took me years to discover myself again. For me to find purpose. Thoughts kept going through my head that I'm meant to help others because of my experience. What? I wasn't ready for over four years. Instead, I continued a business that I wanted to exit until the pandemic brought that to a screeching halt. In many ways I knew it was time to move on. I lovingly call this time my floundering year. I would get involved with something then find that it didn't excite me. So, I'd move onto something else. And so, it continued.

Once I was ready, I became a certified master grief coach to help others along the grieving process and discover who they are now without their loved one. I found a part of me was willing to come out. It's satisfying to be able to help others. I finally realized that I was being selfish by not offering my gifts of compassion and understanding to others. We can all use our experience to be of service even if all we can give is a smile. That smile can cause a chain reaction.

I continue to learn how different we each are by assisting my clients along their journey. I find that one of the biggest reasons they seek out a coach or therapist is to be able to share their story. I find that many people who are grieving have never shared their story with anyone. It's important to have support from friends and loved ones. Professionals can be of assistance when more support is required.

I leave you with a story of signs from the other side. It was the following spring after Nate's passing that I noticed a plant popping out of the ground in front of our home. Normally I would just pull it out thinking it was a weed. Something told me to wait and see what it is as it gets bigger. I was so happy that I did! It turns out that it was sunflowers! One of my favorite flowers! To me it's a happy flower. I took this as a sign from Nate because we had never planted any seeds. It's important to believe. It makes me smile thinking of it.

My hope is that my story along with the other author's stories in this book inspires you to find a way to be happy in those moments in between grief. I believe there's a lesson in everything. Even in the tragedy of loss our light can continue to shine through in places. Our memories live on in our minds and hearts forever. Love is eternal.

Shining A Light on Grief is to help bring a taboo subject out in the open. May your light shine brightly into the future along with mine to make a difference for all who go through their own journey of grief.

Made in USA - Kendallville, IN
98936_9781958217191
09.12.2022 1422